34 MILLION FRIENDS

of the women of the world

Jane Roberts

Jane Roberts (signature)

Lady Press

Sonora California
USA

51795

9 781889 409344

34 MILLION FRIENDS   SOCIOLOGY-WOMEN

COVER DESIGN:
Georgia Jones
FRONT COVER PHOTO:
On the Way to the Market
Burkina-Faso, Yatenga province
Photographer: Marie Dorigny
BACK COVER PHOTO:
William A. Ryan/UNFPA
Other photographs in this book are from the collection of Jane Roberts and UNFPA.

The views expressed in this publication are those of the author(s) and do not necessarily represent the views of UNFPA, the United Nations or any of its affiliated organizations, including Americans for UNFPA.
Copyright ©2005
Jane Roberts
Printed in the United States of America
Library of Congress Cataloguing in Publication Data   2005932244
Jane Roberts, author
34Million Friends of the women of the world
ISBN 1-889409-34-0

A donation from the sale of this book is being made to 34 Million Friends

To my family and to all who are of woman born.

INDEX

Acknowledgements

You are reading this book because I had help. Let me offer heart-felt thanks to:

Lois Abraham, who showed me the power of two.

Stirling Scruggs who has climbed out on many limbs for us!

Kakenya Ntaiya for being willing to share her story.

Vernon Mack for saying, "Why not!"

Thoraya Obaid, Executive Director of UNFPA, champion of the women of the world and of 34 Million Friends.

UNFPA in the persons of Sarah Craven, Abubakar Dungus, Kristin Hetle, Alvaro Serrano, Mari Tikkanen, Micol Zarb and many more for making this book possible.

Americans for UNFPA who encouraged me no end.

Nils Daulaire, M.D., of the Global Health Council for speaking out. The UN Foundation without whom there wouldn't be a "Travel" chapter.

David Harwood and Ellen Marshall who "fact checked".

Jerome Friedman and Linda Harrar for friendship.

Elena Cabatu of CCMC for keeping me informed.

Jay Roberts who edits and proof reads like a fiend.

Georgia Jones of LadybugPress for her very big leap of faith in saying YES before even seeing a manuscript.

Contributors to 34 Million Friends without whom there certainly would be no story!

Jane Roberts

34 MILLION FRIENDS

of the women of the world

INTRODUCTION
Kakenya Ntaiya

 *I met Kakenya Ntaiya in 2004 at the Global Health Council Conference in Washington, D.C. I was fortunate to appear with her later at Scripps College in Claremont, California. I asked her to contribute her story to this book because I have such profound admiration and respect for this young woman. Her story serves as a background for everything that is in this book. Please read on.*

One Girl's Story

I was born and grew up in a Maasai community 250 miles west of Nairobi, the capital of Kenya. I am the first of eight siblings. Maasai tradition requires that a child, especially a girl, do chores by age five, collecting firewood, milking cows, fetching water from the river, and herding cows. I was no exception, and as the oldest I also had to help my mother raise my siblings.

My father worked as a policeman in Nairobi and sometimes did not come home for a year or more. My mother had to raise us all by herself. Most days we slept without food; my mother was herding two cows and did not do any farming. We worked on other peoples' farms in order to earn money to buy food, clothes, and school supplies, including notebooks, pens, uniforms, school fees and all other school expenses. But we could earn only about 50 shillings, less than one US dollar per day. It was a hard task, working on someone else's farm at such an early age; sometimes I did not weed correctly, and before I got paid I had to repeat the work.

Whenever my father came home to visit, he would sell the few cows my mother had raised and use the money for drinking with his friends. When my mom complained, my father would beat her, because according to our traditions all the family's wealth belongs to the man. A woman owns nothing. My mother would run away and stay with her family until my father left. While she was gone, life was hard for me and my little siblings. We had to do all the duties that my mother performed. We cried a lot until he went away again and our mom came back to us.

What I saw at home made me to yearn for a different life. I kept asking myself, "I am just helping my mother—what is going to happen to me when I have to raise my own child all by myself?" This question made me search for something better. I wanted to have my own wealth, my own lifestyle. My mother told me, "I do not want you to live the life I am living." She wanted me to be different, and the only way I could see to achieve this was to do well in school and become a teacher.

My teachers were my role models. Most of them came from other communities. My belief then was that teaching was not as hard as working in the fields on a hot day with a stern supervisor. Teachers wore different clothes and shoes every day—they were neat. They seemed to be happy all the time; they spoke in English. This was the life I wanted.

My dreams may seem small to others, something that could be achieved with no problem. But this was not the case for me or other girls in my village with dreams of a better life. I was engaged when I was less than five years old. The groom's family and my extended family made the arrangements – the ties were signified by a chain that the groom put around my neck. My family was very happy, because if I was engaged it proved my mother was hard-working and my family had good values.

Because of my engagement, my teachers did not believe I could do well in school and become a teacher one day; they never paid attention or encouraged me. They knew I was supposed to get married as soon as I underwent female circumcision—this is the rite of passage to adulthood in the Maasai community. At home I did not have time to study because in the evening I had to help my mother, who was tired from her day's work. We do not have electricity, and at night I was not allowed to use the one little paraffin lamp we had because the paraffin would run out too soon. This meant I did not study at night. I only studied in school, so I prayed to God to help me pass my exams so that I could become a teacher.

My biggest supporter was my mother, even though she sometimes beat me to discipline me. She meant well; she always told me, "I don't want you to live the life I am living." She was very protective of me against men and boys. Many girls were getting pregnant at an early age and my mother didn't want that to happen. She told me to stay away from men, saying, "They will make you pregnant, then laugh at you and leave you to suffer alone." I also knew that if I got pregnant it would shame my family and my mother would be blamed. Some girls in my village died trying to perform abortions. Most would use roots from a bush, some used a clothes detergent called "Omo," and others tried many other traditional techniques. Whenever my mother saw me walking with a man she would beat me. So I learned to stay away from men— except in school, where I learned a lot from them.

The first big challenge to my dream came after I finished primary school, when I was fourteen years old. I was supposed to undergo female circumcision, a process I now refer to as female genital mutilation. I knew that once I underwent this process, I was going to get married, because this is the passage to adulthood. My idea was to postpone getting circumcised as long as possible, because as long as I was not circumcised, no one would want to marry me. I asked my father to postpone the rite of passage until my primary school national exam results came out. We negotiated and agreed that if I did well, I could go on to secondary school, and if not I would get married.

Thank God, when December came and the results were out, I had done well, and my father had to keep his promise by agreeing I could go to secondary school. Everybody in my village was happy for me and bought my father beer for the celebration. He told me that he was going to Nairobi to find me the best high school in the city and would come back for me in a month.

The school term started at the end of February, but my father did not come back. I told my mother he was not going to come and I needed to go to school. She went to the nearest boarding school in my area, the Sosio Secondary School in Kilgoris, and asked the headmaster if I could join. Since I had done fairly well in my primary exams, he accepted. The next challenge was to find money for school fees and materials. We had some money from farming but it was not enough, so my mother promised the head teacher to pay the rest as soon as she could.

I continued with school until the April short vacation, and went home with my first term test results. My mother was very happy—I had done well and did not let her down. But my father was not happy that I had gone to school without his permission. He had arranged for the genital cutting ceremony to take place in a week. I did not know what to do. Finally I told my father I would only go through the ceremony if he let me go back to school. At first he did not know how to respond, and then he started yelling at me. If I was not circumcised it would be a disgrace to him and my entire family. But I was determined. This was the only thing I had that I could hold on to, because as long as I was not circumcised no man would want to marry me. Finally, we agreed. I would be circumcised and then I could go back to school.

The following week I went through the genital circumcision process. It was very painful—you are not given any painkiller and you have to act brave. You are not allowed to cry, and it is torture. But in three weeks, I was back to school. I healed quickly because my mother went against tradition and brought a nurse in secret to give me some medication against infection. I was very lucky.

During my second year in high school my father had the first of a series of strokes that eventually left him completely paralyzed. I spent a lot of time talking with him in the hospital, and we completely resolved all our differences. He told me to take care of our family and that he trusted me with all I was doing. He also told me that he had wanted me to get married because he was getting pressure from my uncles. But he told me I was free to do whatever I wanted to do.

My dream of coming to America to get an education started during high school. A guy by the name of Morompi Ole Ronkei from my village had gone to America and studied at the University of Oregon. He came back to the village dressed in jeans, white T-shirt and sneakers, and he had a camera on his shoulder. I admired that lifestyle, and he seemed happy every time I saw him. I told him I also wanted to come to America and get an education as he did. At first he thought I was joking, because I was already engaged and there was no way I was going to leave my husband-to-be and go to America—no girl in my village had ever done that. But then he saw how determined I was and how I negotiated to finish secondary school and stay unmarried.

He told me he would talk to his friend Kathleen Bowman who was president of a woman's college—Randolph Macon Woman's College in Lynchburg, Virginia. He got me the admission forms and I was accepted. At the same time I had applied to the Teachers' College in Kenya and also got accepted there. I had to decide which college to attend. The teachers' college was much cheaper, and in three years I would finish and be able to help my mother and my little siblings. The American college was very expensive and far away from home, but the minute I got the Randolph-Macon acceptance letter, I knew I was going to America. I chose the hardest road because I knew that after I was done with it, I would reap greater fruits.

Now I needed to raise money for my visa, passport, airfare, and tuition. In this I needed the support of my entire community—not just their financial support, but blessings from the elders. According to our traditions, a child does not just belong to the father and the mother but to the clan as whole. Most people didn't understand what it meant to say I was going to America to get a college education. I already had a husband, and why was I going away? No one wanted to support me at first. No girl in my village had ever left to go to America. So I had to use the culture to convince the elders to support me. According to our traditions, if you go to someone's house in the morning before sunrise, they cannot say no to you because something bad will happen if they do. I used this technique by going very early to visit one elder called Ongoni, who is known for getting things done. I told him I needed his help in fundraising to help me go to America. He had no option but to say yes. He gave me a list of another sixteen elders, and I did the same early-morning visits to them. They all agreed and came together to help me.

I also wanted the support of the village women. I told them that if they supported me I would come back from America and help them achieve whatever they wanted. They discussed this and gave me a list of the things they needed most.

They wanted to build a maternity clinic because so many women in my village had died during pregnancy. No hospital is nearby that they can go to when they have complications giving birth. Everyone gives birth at home with the help of other women and grandmothers. They also wanted a girls' school, because many girls were getting pregnant in primary school. The mothers were being blamed, but it wasn't their fault, and they wanted to separate their daughters at school from the boy students who just wanted to sleep with them and impregnate them. I told them I would do these things if they supported me. So at the end, everyone in my village came together and raised enough money to send me to America to get an education.

My challenges were great but with God I was able to make it. Two scriptures in the Bible were my source of encouragement: "Jesus said unto him, If thou canst believe, all things are possible to him that believeth." (Mark 9:23), and "And Jesus looking upon them saith, With men it is impossible, but not with God: for with God all things are possible." (Mark 10:27).

In May of 2004, I graduated with a Bachelor of Arts Degree in International Studies and Political Science from Randolph-Macon Woman's College in Lynchburg, Virginia. This was a proud moment I shared with my mother and her friend who came to America for the ceremony. Although my education has brought me to the United States, I plan to go back home and help women and children attain their goals.

Since September 2004, I have had the privilege of working for UNFPA, the United Nations Population Fund, as youth advisor. I learned about the United Nations system in college where I took part in a Model United Nations, and I always wanted to work for the UN. I was introduced to UNFPA in June 2004 when I was invited to speak about child marriage at the Global Health Council meeting. I told my life story as I have told it above, and mentioned that I was looking for a job. The Communications Consortium Media Center (CCMC) in Washington employed me to work and speak on population issues and genital mutilation, and later I moved to UNFPA.

Working for UNFPA has made me broaden my ideas and increased my desire to help women around the world. I made a promise to return to my village, and I am going to do that, because all that I have always wanted to teach my village is in the kind of work that UNFPA does. I know I can be useful at home through helping the village women get a clinic and a girls' school, and also by being a role model for other young girls. I want them to achieve their goals without having to bargain with their parents about their education. I want them to know that the sky is the limit and that they can be whatever they want to be. I know that marriage is a blessed institution, but if girls get married at an early age, they will not be happy.

UNFPA's larger goal is to advance the goals agreed on by governments that met in 1994 at the International Conference on Population and Development (ICPD). Some of the ICPD goals include helping girls go to school and working with community and religions leaders to find alternatives to female genital mutilation. Studies show that in the next decade, 130 million girls will undergo this terrible procedure as I did—and I would like to help eliminate this practice so no one ever has to go through it again.

UNFPA is also working at many levels to ensure that girls do not get married before their 18th birthday, and that married adolescents have safe pregnancies and delivery. They also want to ensure that young people are involved in decision-making, because to have leaders tomorrow you have to train them today. To help in these goals, UNFPA has two creative initiatives for youth at its headquarters in New York: the Youth Advisory Panel (YAP) and the Special Youth Program (SYP). The YAP brings young people age 15 to 24 from around the globe to advise the organization on how best to serve youth. SYP recruits young people from developing countries to come to New York for six months to help plan and evaluate UNFPA youth programs in their own countries.

Every intern is encouraged to develop a program that focuses on their region or country. At the end of the time in New York, interns spend three months at a UNFPA country office implementing their ideas.

It is time for us young people to realize that our efforts today can change the future. We have to be involved in creating policies that affect us now in order to make tomorrow better. It is my prayer that as young people we can unite around the globe and take action on these issues—issues that affect us. It is up to us to chase our dreams and to take a stand now for what we believe in. I want everyone in my community to act and live happily, and I hope all young people will do the same in their own communities. We must think globally but act locally, as the saying goes, because whatever we do at home can affect the rest of the world. I think my life so far is proof that we are all connected in one way or another.

Top: Jane meets with villagers who explain how UNFPA community based health workers had helped reduced maternal and infant deaths in their village. Bottom: An elementary school where the children put on a Family Life Education skit for Jane.

Chapter 1
What's at Stake?

Hello, let's chat...

Let's chat about two subjects extremely closely related that are the most important in the world. The first is the fate of the girls and women of the world. The second subject is the issue of population and development. My ultimate goal is a worldwide grassroots movement dedicated to ensuring the full humanity and individual rights of women and girls. This is too important an issue to leave to governments alone. Many are doing a terrible job. The outcome will affect us all. We all must do our part. It's time to take a stand!

This book is in large measure the anatomy of a grassroots movement called 34 Million Friends, the end result of which is absolutely unknown. It may fizzle. On the other hand, it may flourish.

My vision is that a worldwide movement will grow out of 34 Million Friends. In this book, I want to share with you what Lois Abraham and I have been doing for the past three years, and to show you how individuals, working together, can make a difference.

Not in my wildest dreams did I ever think that I would have done the things I've done. Not in my wildest dreams did I ever think I'd be writing a book. This is a very personal book but some wonderful people, Lois, Kakenya, Stirling, Vernon have added their voices.

There will be about 9 billion people on the planet by 2050, up from about 6.4 billion today and up from about 3 billion in 1940. Remember that 1 billion is 1000 million! This growth will come in the poorest countries where there are now huge numbers and percentages of young people. These human beings will be migrating to the cities by the millions, cities whose infrastructures are already straining. On a worldwide scale, I think this will be a humanitarian disaster, an environmental disaster and a threat to peace and stability. On a worldwide scale, there will be conflicts over resources, particularly water, food, and probably energy. I think conflicts over religious beliefs within and between countries are likely to increase.

The most humane, acceptable, partial but crucial answer to what lies ahead is to change the fate of the girls and women of the world. It is to give each and every girl and woman full access to human rights and individual choice in every sphere of human activity. I've been given permission to share part of an article entitled "Saving Girls Should Top World Agenda" by Joan Holmes, President of the Hunger Project. It appeared at Women's eNews on December 14, 2004:

Saving Girls Should Top World Agenda
by Joan Holmes, President, The Hunger Project

"Around the world, girls face the threat of violence, are victims of infanticide, denied healthcare, kept out of school, forced into sexual relations and married without consent. Changing all this in 2005 deserves the whole world's resolve.

As we complete 2004 and assess major world issues, we must confront one critical fact: we are doing a terrible job of taking care of our girls.

While there are many countries where girls are cherished and cared for, the vast majority of girls live in countries where this is not so; in countries of the developing world where there is severe discrimination against women and girls.

In much of the developing world, a little girl eats last and least. She is up to three times more likely than boys to suffer malnutrition.

She is often not taken to the doctor when she is sick and she is less likely to be immunized.

Girls are often kept out of school and put to work. Whether at home, in factories, or in the field, little girls are at work. She starts work at a very young age and works from dawn to dusk, proving the adage "A girl is never a child."

If she does go to school, she's still at risk. Rather than being a safe refuge and a source of empowerment, the school situation is often dangerous. This is the life of a girl in the developing world, if she is allowed to live at all.

Ninety-three million women and girls are "missing" from the world population because of sex-selective abortion, female infanticide, malnutrition, abuse and neglect of female children. Dr. Amartya Sen, Nobel Prize Laureate, coined the term "missing women" to describe the great numbers of women in the world who are literally not alive due to family neglect and discrimination. This is roughly equivalent to all the deaths in all the wars of the 20th century; the most violent century in human history. This is a holocaust many times over.

So why don't we as citizens hear of this tragedy? What kind of world are we living in where 93 million lives can be extinguished just because they're girls? Where's our shame? Where's our moral outrage?

The mistreatment of girls affects us all. The developing world faces problems that affect the entire global community: hunger, poverty, HIV/AIDS and population growth. The developing world also has the most severe discrimination against women and girls. These facts are not unrelated. This severe discrimination against women and girls is a primary cause of the persistence of these problems.

Gender discrimination is the greatest moral challenge of our age. And, we will be judged by history on how we respond to this challenge."

As I read this I kept saying "*Yes*" and "*Yes*" some more. There has been a willful denial of girls' and women's full humanity by individuals, governments, religions, cultures, and customs. This must change, not only because it is the right thing to do, but also because without change there is no chance for either human beings or the planet to thrive. You may not believe this right now, it may seem extreme, but I hope to convince you that a grassroots movement for the girls and women of the world is what the world needs more than anything else to ensure the future. We have a long way to go.

We have to imagine a world where all people, men and women, in equal partnership, with no artificial legal, cultural, religious or economic barriers, work together for the greater good. We must imagine a world where all people regardless of their gender are judged, as Dr. Martin Luther King might have said, only by the content of their character. I must repeat that we have a long way to go.

The United Nations Population Fund, known as UNFPA for the acronym of its former name, United Nations Fund for Population Activities, is in the forefront of this struggle. In over 135 countries it attempts to ensure that women survive childbirth and that they give birth to healthy children. Can you imagine giving birth with nothing but a small sterile plastic sheet, a bar of soap, a razor blade to cut the umbilical cord and string to tie it off? And yet UNFPA distributes these "safe-birth kits" by the thousands in remote villages where they serve as the only midwife. That kit of course is only a small part of their safe motherhood activities.

For the last 30 years the number of maternal deaths from pregnancy related causes has ranged between 500,000 and 600,000 per year. This is more than one per minute. Stephen Lewis, UN Special Envoy for HIV/AIDS in Africa whom I will quote later on AIDS says: "You can bet that if there was something called paternal mortality, the numbers wouldn't be frozen in time for three decades."

UNFPA also offers family planning so that women and their families can choose the number and spacing of their children the way most people do in the developed world. Three hundred fifty million couples in the world lack modern methods of family planning. Family planning is such a gift! UNFPA's mission is family planning. It does not consider abortion a method of family planning and does not perform abortions. Remember that as you read this book.

I hope you are shocked when I tell you that there is a worldwide shortage of family planning commodities. How short-sighted! It's probably a question of there not being big profits in the business. From what I understand, the world could use 10 billion condoms a year yet manufacturers only produce between 3 and 4 billion. Sleep on that little factoid!

As a leader in the effort to bring equality to women and girls, UNFPA especially champions girls' access to education. I will talk more about this later in the description of my trip to Senegal and Mali.

UNFPA plays an integral role in UN-AIDS. More and more, AIDS has a woman's face. Millions of children are losing their mothers, mothers who have played by all the rules and who yet are victims of this scourge.

In April 2005, Stephen Lewis spoke at a Summit on Global Issues in Women's Health in Philadelphia. He said: "What we have here is the most ferocious assault ever made by a communicable disease on women's health, and there is just no concerted coalition of forces to go to the barricades on women's behalf." And later: "The political leadership of Africa has to be lobbied with an almost maniacal intensity or nothing will change." (I would say political leadership everywhere.) Read these words by Stephen Lewis:

"Women have received parity on the receiving end of conflict and AIDS but nowhere else. I see the evidence in the unremitting carnage of women and AIDS. God, it tears the heart from the body. I just don't know how to convey it. These young young women, who crave so desperately to live, who suddenly face a pox, a scourge which tears their life from them before they have a life, who can't even get treatment because the men are first in line, or the treatment rolls out at such a such a paralytic snail's pace, who carry the entire burden of care even while they're sick, tending to the family, carrying the water, tilling the fields, looking after the orphans—the women who lose their property, and have no inheritance rights, and no legal or jurisprudential infrastructure which will guarantee those rights. No criminal code will stop the violence. Because I have observed all of that, and have observed it for four years, and am driven to distraction by the recognition that it will continue, I want a kind of revolution in the world's response."

I say, not a "kind of revolution" but a REVOLUTION.

UNFPA battles the epidemic of violence against women and girls whether it be through female genital mutilation, domestic abuse, rape used as a weapon of war, or early marriage forced upon girls of 12, 13, 14.

Doesn't early marriage do violence to the girl child? At the Global Health Council conference in Washington D.C. in 2004, UNFPA's Executive Director, Thoraya Obaid, presented a new film produced by UNFPA entitled "Too Brief a Child: Voices of Married Adolescents." Heartrending!

I have seen pictures of the effects of female genital mutilation with the resulting scar tissue making it almost impossible for the woman or girl to pee let alone be capable of normal sexual intercourse. I recommend the film "Moolaadé," the story of an African village dealing with one woman who refuses to let her daughter be circumcised. It has played in a very limited number of theaters.

Obstetric fistula is an injury occurring fairly frequently when young girls go into protracted labor with no trained birth attendant. Lois talks in great detail about this scourge in Chapter 2. Oprah Winfrey has taken on obstetric fistula as a cause. UNFPA is launching a worldwide effort to end fistula. If you don't read another word in this book, please visit www.endfistula.org.

And of course when a tsunami strikes and health infrastructures are decimated and there are 150,000 pregnant women who need assistance, UNFPA is there doing what it can.

I was watching like a hawk in 2002, when the Bush Administration made its decision on whether or not to release the $34 million Congress had approved for UNFPA. To me it was the measure of this self-described compassionate conservative. He did not measure up.

Ever since the Reagan years, Republican administrations have used the despicable (my word) Kemp-Kasten amendment to defund UNFPA supposedly because of UNFPA's presence in China, where there are admittedly human rights violations in the government's population policies. Stirling Scruggs explains the ins and outs of this in his chapter, but I want it said that no other country finds fault with UNFPA in this regard.

Any fair interpretation would be that the decision is for domestic consumption, feeding the appetites of the religious right and the anti-UN base of the Republican Party. Add to this the fact that in 2001 the Administration released the congressional allocation with Kemp-Kasten in place and the fact that it contracted with UNFPA to offer reproductive health care in Afghanistan after the US take-over. How could anyone regard this 2002 decision as anything but politics? *Ugly*!

And did you know that any US funds given to UNFPA have always gone into a special account and are never used in China? So to be blunt, we are just hurting the girls and women of the rest of the world, depriving them of the lifesaving, life affirming services of UNFPA. This does great harm to our reputation in the world.

I knew I had to do something when the decision came down from Secretary of State Colin Powell on July 22, 2002. A letter to my Congressman, Jerry Lewis, a silver-haired, Republican party loyalist who, to be charitable, is wishy-washy on these issues, wasn't enough. An LTE which stands for Letter to the Editor (jargon I later learned) wasn't enough either. A brainstorm came to me at 3 a.m. as I lay awake, anger simmering in my brain. Why not, I said to myself, ask 34 million of my fellow Americans to chip in $1. There must be, I reasoned, 34 million Americans who appreciate their contraceptive choices and doctors in the delivery room, 34 million who would chip in a dollar. With that decided, my brain calmed down and I went to sleep.

Well, I did write an LTE to six newspapers, only one of which published it, the *Sun* in San Bernardino, California. This was in late July 2002 and it read:

"A week has passed since the Bush Administration decided to deny the $34 million voted by the Congress for the United Nations Population Fund. Ho Hum, this is vacation time. Columnists have written about it and newspapers have printed editorials of lament. Ho Hum. More women die in childbirth in a few days than terrorism kills people in a year. Ho Hum. Some little girl is having her genitals cut with a cactus needle. Ho Hum that's just a cultural thing. As an exercise in outraged democracy, would 34 million of my fellow citizens please join me by sending one dollar each to the US Committee for UNFPA? That would right a terrible wrong, buy back Colin Powell's soul, and drown out the Ho Hums."

How's that for an LTE! I sent my regular $500 check to the US Committee for UNFPA (now called Americans for UNFPA). I hope Americans for UNFPA becomes just as well known as the US Fund for UNICEF! I also included a one dollar bill saying that I was going to try to get 34 million Americans to do the same. I think they were a little shocked and wrote me a strange letter saying this was not their usual method of fundraising or some such thing. They seemed to think that I was asking them to do it. Which I wasn't! Anyway, it was all straightened out when they talked to UNFPA who had heard from a Lois Abraham with the same idea.

When I received that rather strange letter though, I'll admit that my first reaction was: "Tough, you're going to start getting dollar bills anyway!" I'm a little stubborn that way. And that is how 34 Million Friends started for me.

Above:
34 Million Friends press conference in Dakar, Senegal

Chapter 2
When Abstractions become Personal
by Lois Abraham

In the spring of 2002, this then 68 year old wife, mother, and grandmother got a lesson in women's reproductive health from an unlikely source: *New York Times* columnist Nicholas Kristof. Kristof wrote an article describing the life—or perhaps more accurately, the deprivation of life—of a teenage girl afflicted with obstetric fistula. I had never heard of obstetric fistula.

Although the site of the Waldorf Astoria was once a hospital for its treatment, thanks to the basic health care available to most Americans obstetric fistula has been a medical rarity in the United States for nearly 100 years. The condition is painful to read about and almost unimaginable to live with. It occurs during extremely prolonged labor—often the result of an immature girl attempting to give birth without skilled medical attention. The baby's head, trapped in a too-small birth canal, presses for days against the soft tissue of the vagina. Eventually the pressure cuts off the blood supply, and the tissues die. Fissures or holes form between the vagina and the bladder or rectum, and urine or feces or both constantly leak through the vagina.

The baby is usually stillborn, and the woman becomes an out-cast. The stench that accompanies her everywhere prevents her from living or working in her community.

There was some good news in Mr. Kristof's article. The condition can be cured by surgery. The United Nations Population Fund was spearheading efforts in developing nations both to prevent obstetric fistula by increasing access to basic maternal healthcare and to cure it, in the long run, by making the surgery available to the more than 2 million women worldwide living with the condition. For around $300 the life of a woman suffering from obstetric fistula could literally be bought back.

At the time I read the article I was generally aware of the invaluable work of the United Nations Population Fund, and I also knew that the US contribution of $34 million to the fund had been put on hold and was in danger of being rescinded. The US contribution, according to the Population Fund, could prevent 2 million unwanted pregnancies, nearly 800,000 abortions, 4,700 maternal deaths, nearly 60,000 serious maternal illnesses, as well as over 77,000 infant and child deaths. The very scope of those huge numbers, however, built a barrier of abstraction around them. It is hard to identify with 2 million people. But the Kristof article brought the work of the Population Fund out of the insulating distance of all those numbers and humanized it in the compelling struggle of one horribly hurt young woman.

I have seven grandchildren. One of them is a sixteen year old girl. My experience with my grandchildren has taught me that all of us on Earth are more alike than we are different. I cherish my grandchildren, and more than anything else I want them to grow up safe and healthy. I know that around the world other mothers and grandmothers (and fathers and grandfathers) want their children to grow up safe and healthy too.

So, when the US reneged on its commitment to provide $34 million to the UN Population Fund, I took it personally. The question of the US contribution to the Population Fund was imperative. The 34 Million Friends campaign was the result.

I drafted a chain letter and enlisted friends around the country who committed to sending it to their e-mail lists. Then I made a cold call to UNFPA, leaving a voice message saying I had an idea for raising $34 million and requesting a call back if anyone was interested. Within an hour my call was returned by Vernon Mack, who asked what he could do to help. I told him I needed three things: approval of the draft letter; a safe address to receive money; and an understanding that if the effort was successful, there would be an accounting mess—dollar bills would come pouring in.

Vernon and his assistant, Mari Tikkanen, responded to those needs immediately, and the next day we were set to go! My friends and I pushed our collective "Send" buttons, and the following letter hit thousands of inboxes at once:

Dear Friends:

I am asking you to join in sending a message from 34,000,000 American women. The message will help women living in countries where the lack of medical services (not to mention the lack of other necessities that we take for granted every day) results in hardships beyond our imagination.

The US made a commitment of $34 million to the United Nations Population Fund last winter, with Congress approving the funds and President Bush signing the bill containing the appropriation. The Fund provides family planning and reproductive health services to women in 142 countries. It has a budget of about $270 million worldwide and does "invaluable work," as Secretary of State Colin Powell said during his confirmation hearings. The Fund's programs help some of the most impoverished and underserved women in the world.

Our country has reneged on its commitment. The reason given for refusing to release the $34 million is that the Fund provides aid to Chinese government agencies that force women to have abortions.

However, a State Department fact-finding mission was sent to China in May to investigate exactly that allegation. The mission reported that it found no evidence that the program "knowingly supported or participated in the management of a program of coercive abortion or involuntary sterilization" and recommended that the funds be released. In addition, the Population Fund is barred by law from using US money in China and, as a UN organization, from funding any abortion related activities.

If 34,000,000 American women send one dollar each to the UN Population Fund, we can help the Fund continue its "invaluable work" and at the same time confirm that providing family planning and reproductive health services to women who would otherwise have none is a humanitarian issue, not a political one.

PLEASE, NOW: Put a dollar, wrapped in a plain sheet of paper, in an envelope marked "34 Million Friends." If you wish your name to appear among contributors on the www.unfpa.org web site, write it on the piece of paper. Then mail it today. **EVEN MORE IMPORTANT**: Send this letter on to at least ten friends—more would be better!—who may join in this message.

Thanks,
Lois Abraham

I had no idea where this effort would go. Taking action involves some risk of failure. I have more than once heard that $34 million is an impossibly large number. As one reporter put it, "What led you to decide to tilt at this particular windmill?"

We had early and exciting hints from around the country that the chain letter was multiplying in cyberspace as we had intended, and then the trickle of response began. The trickle became a flood of contributions, often accompanied by warm notes of encouragement and support for the work of the Population Fund.

Also, early on Vernon and Mari learned that there was someone else out there trying to raise money—Jane Roberts. The UNFPA put us together. It was very good to have company!

This experience has reminded me of some very important things: My friends are wonderful, responding way beyond reasonable expectations to get 34 Million Friends launched. It is a privilege but also a responsibility to live in a country where citizens can join grass roots efforts and express dissent freely, and where individuals can take advantage of the incredible technological tools available to get a message out.

Finally, in a time when cynicism seems fashionable, I have met an extraordinary group of people working at the UN Population Fund. They are dedicated and inspiring. It has been particularly rewarding to me to that half of the first $1,000,000 we raised went to "fistula" and that now UNFPA's Fistula Campaign receives a portion of on-going contributions.

And thank you, Mr. Kristof for making the abstract personal!

Lois Abraham

Lois at home in Taos, NM
Photos by Alvaro Serrano, provided by UNFPA

16~34 Million Friends

Chapter 3
The Story from the Inside
by Stirling Scruggs and Vernon Mack

Stirling Scruggs, now retired, was in 2002 and until his retirement in 2004 Director of the Information, Executive Board and Resource Mobilization Division of UNFPA.

When President Bush decided not to release congressionally appropriated funds to UNFPA in 2002, his second year in office, I was disappointed and depressed. Even though Reagan and George H. W. Bush had routinely refused to release UNFPA funding each year, this Bush seemed different. He allowed the release of funds his first year in office and Secretary of State, Colin Powell, spoke highly of UNFPA during his congressional testimony.

But New Jersey Congressman Chris Smith with Chairman Henry Hyde's blessing held hearings in the House Foreign Affairs Committee in which, quite frankly, a fringe group was allowed to present false charges about UNFPA's program in China. If this fringe group's charges had been true, then no country would fund UNFPA. UNFPA would be going against its mandate from the world community and against its whole philosophy.

President Bush sent an expert team to China to investigate, as did the British Parliament and the UN itself. All came back with essentially the same message: "UNFPA is doing good human rights based work and should receive funding." Even a conservative MP from the British team who had introduced legislation in the House of Commons to stop UNPFA funding, was quoted in an interview with the Washington Times as saying, "I have changed my mind about UNFPA, it is a force for good in China."

There were several editorials from around the country condemning the President's decision. This was encouraging, but it was soon over. Then came Jane Roberts and Lois Abraham. Independently both women had come up with the idea of asking 34 million Americans to send at least one dollar each to reach out to women around the world.

Some in UNFPA were doubtful about such a grassroots effort. They thought it would last a few weeks and that the two women would tire and it would end quickly. That is until bags of mail started piling up at UNFPA's mail room. Vernon Mack, the head of UNFPA fundraising and Peter Purdy, head of the US Committee (now Americans for UNFPA) quickly got organized. There were mail opening lunches where staff from all over UNFPA and the US Committee would give up their lunch hours to open letters. Every afternoon Vernon would go down to the street and hand the day's take over to a Brinks truck for delivery to UNFPA's bank. With news in the papers about this effort, I didn't want anyone from UNFPA just walking to the bank with as much as $10,000 in a briefcase.

Within a few weeks, Ted Turner's UN Foundation gave grants to hire staff to handle the mail. UNFPA had promised that 100% of the funds that came in would go to fund programs.

34 Million Friends has given thousands of Americans an opportunity to tell the world that Americans care about the world's women and about the United Nations. Among the letters that arrived my favorite was from a man who wrote, "This $5 is in

honor of the women in my life, my mother, my wife, my two daughters, and my granddaughter."

Jane and Lois are wonderful women who have worked very hard for the last three years. This book tells their wonderful story.

UNFPA community based health workers with suitcases of supplies

Vernon Mack worked in the office of Resource Mobilization and got Lois' famous phone call.

For me, 34 Million Friends started one late morning in July 2002. A woman from New Mexico called me out of the blue. Lois Abraham said she had followed the news about the Bush Administration's decision to withdraw funding for UNFPA and she was upset and concerned. She was so concerned that she wanted to do something and asked me if UNFPA could accept contributions from individuals.

UNFPA had over the years received unsolicited contributions from individuals as well as from organizations. One year we received a $400 check from a Baptist Church in Little Rock, Arkansas, and I had always wondered what prompted them to make a contribution. These unexpected private donations would amount to no more that perhaps $10,000 per year. With a staff of four: two professional officers and two clerical staff, the office of Resource Mobilization had never considered a campaign for private gifts. UNFPA did not have any capability for organizing such an effort. This thought was going through my mind as I talked to Mrs. Abraham.

I did tell her though that we could receive private donations and she said that that was great and then sounded me out about her idea to draft a letter to circulate to her friends over the Internet. We would have to approve the letter first, as she wanted to be entirely accurate in what she said.

I kind of wondered how much money she expected to raise, but thought "what the heck," there would be no transaction costs on our end and there was no reason to say *No*. Let's face it, we knew next to nothing about the capabilities of the Internet for fundraising purposes.

My boss Stirling Scruggs then told me about a Jane Roberts who was contacting organizations with the same idea. This combined effort started what in my mind was one of the most innovative and exciting fundraising initiatives, not only for the UNFPA but as it turned out, for the entire UN system. Who could have dreamed, let alone plan, the positive outcome of using the Internet this way? Who would have thought that this effort by two women would rocket UNFPA into the headlines of several major US newspapers and then across the Atlantic to Europe and then to Japan and Australia?

My most vivid memory is the boxes and boxes of mail and it went on for months. Boy, did we have fun getting all those one dollar bills, and ten and twenty dollar bills and reading the accompanying notes. What a story! — and I really want to thank Mari Tikkanen of my staff for organizing all the very detailed work associated with money counting and record keeping.

I am so glad I was in the office the day that Lois called!

Left: Nyamana, Mali. A UNFPA health worker given micro credit to raise sheep. Right: Children at a joint Mali/UNFPA school in Markacounga, Mali

UNFPA Family Planning Clinic, Mali. FNUAP is UNFPA in French!

Chapter 4
Jane Roberts

I am a 64 year old retired French teacher and tennis coach. A short look at my life might explain how I got to thinking the way I think, so I will try to relate some aspects of my life to my present preoccupations.

I was born on August 27, 1941. My father was a 40 year old English professor at San Diego State College (now SDSU) and my mother was a junior high science and math teacher who didn't work outside the home after I and my sister came along. I actually think my parents were elated to have two girls.

Growing up, I was quite shy, and always a little in the *out* group as opposed to the *in* group all through school. I was known though as an athlete, as I attained a national tennis ranking of 5 for girls 15 and under in 1955. Billie Jean Moffitt (King) was younger than I but a tennis friend of my sister. She stayed at our house at least once for a tournament. She has fought her whole life for women's equality in sports.

For the year 1959-60, my sophomore year in college, my father took the family to France for a sabbatical year. By that time I had had two years of high school and one year of college French.

That year was a wake-up year. French students were debating communism versus capitalism, reading newspapers, and discussing world issues. I was in awe.

A French boyfriend and hard study meant that I was learning the language fast. So I finished a French major at San Diego State in 1962 and in 1963 received an M.A. in Paris studying with the Middlebury College Graduate School of French in France. I slaved. I'll never forget having two hours to prepare for my final oral *explication de texte*, with my head pounding so hard I had to lay it on the desk and hope for the best. Walking out of that room after it was all over, my headache was completely gone. I went to sit in the Jardin du Luxembourg and to smile and smile to myself. I had done it.

I knew that a Ph.D. was not for me. There followed a further year of study at the University of Arizona in Tucson before President George Armacost hired me for the fall of 1964 as an instructor in French at the University of Redlands in Redlands, California.

It was absolutely wonderful to be able to speak fluent French during my visits to Senegal and Mali in 2003. Never have I been more grateful for skill at a foreign language.

In August of 1965, I married Julian Roberts (Jay), an assistant professor of chemistry at Redlands. George Bush would be happy because I had been technically abstinent until my wedding night!

There was a more or less liberal group of young faculty and Jay and I gravitated to this group. In 1968 Dr. Robert Morlan, a giant in the political science department, got me involved in the Redlands Democratic Club and suggested I be a faculty advisor for a brilliant senior, Sue Thomas, who wanted to put together a course on women as an honors project for the university's January interim. Sue and I did a great job and I taught the solidly academic course for 4 interims with over 100 students enrolled each time. Betty Friedan's **The Feminine Mystique** had been published in 1963 and was one of the required readings for the course. Just to give you an idea about the tenor of the times, neither abortion nor lesbianism was covered in the course outline.

By 1971, Jay and I had been using family planning for several years and were ready for kids, really ready! But I couldn't get pregnant in spite of trying everything we could, including taking my temperature, sperm count, tubes blown out, and quite a bit of frustration. Finally realizing that it just wasn't going to happen, we thrillingly and joyfully adopted seven-week-old Jeffrey in February of 1974. Isn't adoption reproductive health care?

And, because this is a very personal book, I want to tell a personal story about a magical moment. Once, when Jeff was a year old, I had him in the bathroom with me and he was standing by the tub while I took a bath. He saw a little leaf in the water, reached in for it and put it right on my nose. Well, I can't tell you how we laughed and laughed and laughed. The joy of parenthood is so great when people are ready to be parents. I wish it so for everyone.

And then in 1975-76 while we were in France on Jay's sabbatical which he spent working with a chemistry professor from the University of Grenoble… something about that French air, anyway, I was pregnant at age 35. Joy and vomiting and prenatal care! And, when Annie was born on September 28, 1976 in Redlands, never has a woman been more grateful for a doctor in the delivery room. Fetal monitor, pain management, lots and lots of attention.

Wow people, I can't imagine doing it by myself; I would have been utterly panicked. Doesn't every woman in the world deserve the same? And knowing that I wasn't going to die in childbirth when one woman dies every minute somewhere on the planet! My goodness. Think about the great gifts of contraception and assisted birth. We take them for granted.

Jeffrey had many ear infections and I could always get him in to see a doctor right away. Annie got the flu once when she was about 10. She literally couldn't walk because her muscles were so affected. I had a doctor to reassure me that it was just the flu. Reassurance from a doctor, what a gift! Think of the women in isolated villages, in poor countries or in huge urban slums whose kids are sick, coughing, pulling on their ears, feverish, whatever. Think of the helplessness of having no real recourse for your sick child. I can't imagine the pain.

Ten million children under the age of 5 die every year. Often they are little bits of things, born too small to survive, or suffering from drinking unclean water, or from disease. That equals ten million mothers with excruciating feelings of helplessness and grief. How is this tolerated? Isn't being able to take your kids to a doctor reproductive health care?

I gave my kids healthy snacks while they watched "Sesame Street". How about the mothers who see their kids going hungry or right now in Niger and Mali starving?

I was very lucky as the kids were growing up. I taught French on a part time basis and gave private tennis lessons and also tennis classes at a community college. So I could earn a little money, which always feels good, and be almost a full time mother. That was a great gift.

And there were times when I was quite politically active, being for several years president of the Redlands Democratic Club and attending in the late seventies the very first March for Women's Lives, a giant pro-choice demonstration in Washington. My whole family marched with me the next weekend in Los Angeles in pouring rain.

Somehow, I developed the philosophy that I would never second guess a woman when it came to her choices about birth control and abortion. I don't want my government second guessing women either.

But that is not the role of the United Nations. Because the world recognizes the UNFPA role in preventing abortions, a record number of countries, 166 to be exact, contributed to UNFPA in

2004. Some countries, Canada for instance, increased their contribution to help make up for our dereliction of duty.

And, did you know that 40 women per minute in the developing world seek an unsafe, usually illegal abortion? These are often mothers of several children, who feel desperate and for whom modern methods of contraception are simply not available. How can we tolerate this? How can we not have access to contraception available for all? Think of the terror—I don't use the word lightly—of a clandestine abortion. My utter conviction is that no woman should have to risk her own life in order to do what she feels is right for herself and her family.

In 1989 with both my parents deceased and my kids in high school, I decided to teach full time, so I got my public school teaching credential and taught French and coached the boys' and girls' tennis teams at Eisenhower High School in Rialto, California from 1990 through 1998. Eisenhower was a tough high school, wonderful kids and terribly mixed-up kids, gangs and urban problems. I suppose my best and worst students were Latinas. Some became almost tri-lingual, speaking English, Spanish, and French at the end of their high school years. Others combed their hair and put on make-up, got pregnant and brought their babies to the high school nursery.

I had some great guy tennis players. For my girls' teams I had to recruit several beginners from the general student body to get the 9 girls I needed. I felt that was very worthwhile, teaching girls who were pretty inactive physically this life long sport. I often think how girls in poor countries miss out on sports. Think of the girls who are all wrapped up at an early age with no chance for organized sports, for competition, for the thrill of the game.

In June 1998, after 38 years as a professor of chemistry at the University of Redlands, my husband retired at age 64 and I quit the high school position. Through the years my interest had shifted from the domestic fight for legal abortion to international population and reproductive health issues. This was what I wanted to spend time on, as well as to learn how to play golf!

And so in 2001, when I heard about the PLANET Campaign funded by the Hewlett and Packard Foundations to try to urge Americans to take an interest in these issues, I was elated. I signed up right away for a Population Activist Weekend in Washington D.C. sponsored by the Sierra Club, the National Audubon Society, the National Wildlife Federation and Population Connection. Others from my area attending this same training were Ladd Seekins, now California Population Chair for the Sierra Club, Drew Feldmann, Melissa Culley, and John Green, all from the National Audubon Society, and Allen Mitchell, a set designer for San Bernardino theater productions. We have all stuck together, and added some more people like Marilyn Hempel who started the Population Coalition within the League of Women Voters and Jean Frederickson, a community educator. We now call ourselves Inland Planet (www.inlandplanet.org) and have sponsored, over the last 5 years, an amazing number of community events and tabled at countless Orange Blossom Festivals, Route 66 celebrations, and Earth Day symposiums.

For me, that Population Activist weekend in Washington was pivotal. The one talk I remember vividly was delivered by Abubakar Dungus from UNFPA. He used this phrase which has stuck with me: "UNFPA works in the sweat and toil of everyday life to bring reproductive health services to the dispossessed of the earth."

That was like a stab in my heart. I knew it was true. And I also knew—and here you will think I'm an egomaniac with delusions of grandeur—that I was probably the one totally lay person who knew more about this, and who cared more about this, and who had thought more about this than any other lay person on the planet and that I should talk to the world about this. ...

Total pipe dream of course! Hmmm. Amazing! I have actually to some extent talked to the world about this, but more about that later.

With that short history of my life I think you can see how I got to where I am. These ideas of having the world get serious about its women and girls have been maturing for over 35 years. And for over 3 years, I have been joyfully relentless in pursuing this search for 34 million friends of the women of the world.

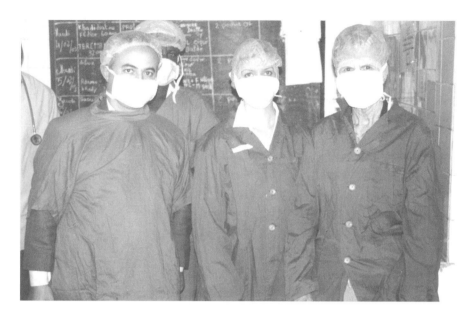

Left to Right: at Le Dantec hospital in Dakar, Alvaro Serrano, Mari Tikkanen and Jane

Left: This man has a store serving several villages thanks to micro-credit. Jane asked him to hold up a box of condoms.
Right: This man goes from village to village singing songs about reproductive health.

Chapter 5
Trying to Find 34 Million Friends

The Activist Weekend was pivotal because, when the announcement of the defunding was made on July 22, 2002, I had the email addresses of about 200 people from around the country who had attended. I emailed them all suggesting the idea of finding 34 million people to chip in at least one dollar. The response was very positive, and I learned that a certain Lois Abraham, not knowing about the US Committee, had contacted the UNFPA directly and that her emails were flying around the World Bank. Frankly, I was a little jealous.

How dare this perfect stranger come up with the same brilliant idea! Ah well, time would tell and just perhaps two heads were better than one. THEY WERE!

I always thought that in order to reach the most people, we had to contact organizations rather than individuals, or at least individuals who could then inform their organizations.

I contacted the League of Women Voters of which I've been a long time member and talked to Executive Director Nancy Tate. She finally agreed to sell me the mailing labels for the nationwide chapters provided that I make it very clear that this was not under any circumstances official LWV business. I was thrilled.

And then one morning… I'm sitting at the breakfast table with my bowl of oatmeal and reading in the sports section of the Los Angeles Times about Augusta National and the Masters Golf Tournament. I also see a blurb about a certain Martha Burk, president of something called the National Council of Women's Organizations and of her fight to open Augusta National to women members.

I race upstairs and google National Council of Women's Organizations (NCWO) and can't believe what I see: One hundred organizations all nominally pro-choice, a total membership of over 6,000,000 women. Hey, you might say, why haven't 6 million women given a dollar? I ask the same thing!

NCWO includes the three I belong to, the League of Women Voters, the American Association of University Women, and Planned Parenthood. It also includes the YWCA, the American College of Nurse-Midwives, the United Methodist Church and on and on. And so, as on so many other days of this campaign, I have lots to do. I jot down all the information, an email address and a phone number. I start off by phoning. They don't know me from Eve of course, but here I am spouting off about this wonderful plan to get 34 million people to give one dollar to the United Nations Population Fund. Luckily, Rebecca in the office is receptive to what must have appeared a little nutty.

She tells me to write Martha, and if I remember correctly, I do. She also tells me that the following week the entire Board of NCWO is meeting and perhaps they could endorse this effort. I am excited. It seems that for a week I play phone tag with Martha. Finally, Rebecca stays home one morning when she has suggested that I call Martha and I think that her staying at home is on purpose so that Martha, who is completely taken up with the Augusta National controversy, will have to answer the phone. Which she does. Whew! We have a nice conversation, the upshot of it being that the Board of NCWO unanimously endorses 34 Million Friends. I view this as a real coup on my part. I'm so proud of myself for being so stubborn and following through. And Martha Burk will take part in the first press briefing for 34 Million Friends in New York in October, 2002.

I get the mailing labels for all the NCWO organizations and then I think to myself, Aha! Women's Studies! That is a natural.

So how in the world do I go about getting information? I think I talk to someone in the University of Redlands Women's Studies area, although my recollection is very vague on this point. I end up calling the Women's Studies Department at the University of Minnesota about 6:30 a.m. my time one morning in order to speak to a specific person and miracle of miracles, she answers the phone. This is in September, 2002. She tells me to look up the National Women's Studies Association, which I find at www.NWSA.org, whose headquarters are at the University of Maryland. By hook and by crook, I find out that there are indeed mailing labels for all the departments nationwide and that a certain Gerri might be able to furnish them to me for a nominal fee. Gerri is a real gem, loves the idea behind 34 MF and gives me a really good price on the mailing labels. And it turns out that she knew about 34 MF already and had sent an email out about it. From her on November 15, 2002: "Fantastic, I know the email is circulating because my own message has already routed back to me several times."

I can't believe my good fortune. But how to pay for sending out all these packets of information and materials? Answer coming up.

By September 2002, envelopes had really started to arrive, Lois' people to UNFPA and mine to the US Committee. And what was really nice was that an anonymous donor from Maine had sent in $25,000 so our total on the web after the first weeks looked a little respectable. The upshot was that the US Committee and UNFPA issued press releases and what's more, invited both Lois and me back to New York in October for a press briefing to give this effort a small publicity boost.

My husband and I had already planned a vacation in New York just at that time in order to support the city after 9/11 so this was perfect. The US Committee was sponsoring a Family of Woman exhibit in the lobby of the UN, the opening for which there was going to be a lovely reception. Lois and I were invited. What's more, we were invited to be on the Honorary Committee for the exhibit. I got the giggles seeing Lois and me listed with Donald Trump, Jean Rather, and Mavis Leno.

—By the way, Mavis Leno and the Feminist Majority Foundation have been heroic in their efforts for Afghan women, but the task is Herculean!

In this news update dated August 16, 2005 on Afghanistan from the United Nations Children's Fund: "About 20% of children in Afghanistan die before their fifth birthday, girls being particularly vulnerable. Girls' enrollment in secondary schools is less than 10%, female illiteracy rates as high as 85%. In some parts of Afghanistan, maternal death rates are as high as 6,000 per 100,000 women. UNICEF is declaring a state of ACUTE EMERGENCY for women and children living in Afghanistan." (I also learned today that UNFPA is reopening six clinics in and around Kabul)

The press briefing was on October 10, 2002 at the Church Center for the United Nations on 1st Ave. at 44th St. Martha Burk had consented to take part as had Carolyn Donovan, the representative from the American Association of University Women to the UN and Ellen Marson, the then president of Hadassah. These women were representing the NCWO. Thoraya Obaid, the Saudi woman, graduate of Mills College in Oakland, California, who was now Executive Director of UNFPA, had wonderfully warm words for Lois and Jane. (Incidentally, Thoraya credits her achieving her present position to her Saudi father for wanting her as a little girl to be educated and free of normal Saudi constraints.)

Lois and I both spoke for 2 or 3 minutes. I know I quoted the following email which had *made my day* at the very beginning of this effort. It was from a Bonnie Lane Webber of New York City and she had written on September 10, 2002, just about 6 weeks after the start: "Jane, did you come up with this idea? It is one of those small, brilliant, wonderful, quiet, moving, ideas that remind me of why I am involved in environmental causes. It is so that ideas like this will come across my radar screen. I just received it email from Frank Eadie of the Sierra Club. I thank you Jane Roberts whoever you are." (After I got back from my Senegal/Mali trip I went to Bonnie's apartment in New York City and spoke to her environmental group, for which she puts out the newsletter entitled *Grassroots*.)

After the press briefing, we attended the very elegant evening reception for the US Committee's Family of Woman Exhibit in the lobby of the UN. I remember three things. First, the beautiful photos depicting women's lives all over the world. If this very moving exhibit comes to your city, go see it. I remember Thoraya calling Lois and me up to be introduced and then having our pictures taken with her, a great honor. And finally, toward the end of the evening, I'm standing with a group of people just chatting and I say: "Boy, I wish I had $5000 to mail all these wonderful packets to all the LWV chapters, NCWO organizations and Women's Studies Departments."

"Oh, I'll give you $5000," says a completely unknown-to-me fellow who turns out to be Walter Coddington of "Face to Face, The Face of Women's Rights," an NGO (non-governmental organization), which has an international group of Goodwill Ambassadors supporting women around the world. More about "Face to Face" later, but there... now I've told you how I got the money for my mailings. And you should have seen my Inland Planet group, on the floor at my house and at the kitchen table, and at card tables addressing and stamping and stuffing envelopes. It was funny!

And a word about Linda Harrar: She has been involved in several documentaries for PBS about the environment, population, and women's empowerment for want of a better word. Somehow, she and I had made email contact. I had invited her down from Boston for the Family of Woman reception and she had squeezed in the trip. So we met and chatted. Now here is someone who has really done wonders for communicating what is at stake!

On April 20, 2004, on PBS, NOVA aired "World in the Balance," Linda Harrar, producer. Throughout this whole campaign whenever 34 Million Friends has had a write-up on Planetwire Clips, she has sent it to me with a "You Go Girl" and I have smiled contentedly. She told me that in the final thank-you's at the end of the Nova Program, my name is listed but that it will go by too fast for me to see. I think we were also a link on the PBS website about this program.

Linda and I have recently discussed doing a documentary about what reproductive health care is all about and emphasizing the need for worldwide grassroots support for the women and girls of the world. I don't think the general public is really aware of the difficulties and complications of bringing reproductive health care to everyone. Yet it must be done.

And it was during this visit to New York that my husband opened an envelope from a woman who had included a check for $310 and written the names of 310 people, relatives and friends from whom she had waylaid a dollar. We try to put all names on the web.

This trip also started our love affair with the Pong Sri restaurant on E. 48th St. in New York City. Serendipitously, the evening after the press briefing, Jay and I walked in there and were eating at a table next to Irwin and Carol Leimas. After I explained to them what we were doing in New York, and that AAUW's

Carolyn Donovan had taken part in the press briefing, Carol Leimas said that she was the former representative of AAUW to the United Nations and knew Carolyn Donovan quite well. The upshot of this was that Carol Leimas and her friend Marsha Handel organized a "Bark For Women Dog Walk" in Central Park in New York City on Sunday, December 8, 2002 with a big turn-out of dogs and people for 34 Million Friends.

And, I opened an envelope from former Senator Alan Simpson, Republican of Wyoming, that contained a check for $100 made out to the US Committee with his address and phone number. Huge nerve on my part but I called and learned that indeed the check was to 34 Million Friends and since that time he and I have talked once or twice. He knows that human numbers are important and that women's rights are a part of the battle. He has endorsed 34 Million Friends. His wonderful letter is on our web site.

Barbara Kingsolver, author of *The Poisonwood Bible*, *Prodigal Summer*, and *Pigs in Heaven* was also an early supporter.

And I must say that we had to change our flights to and from New York several times in order to arrive later, stay longer. I remember explaining to a Southwest Airlines telephone reservation woman (fairly young, I would judge) the reason for these numerous changes and her referring to what we were asking for 34 Million Friends as "just the price of a soda."

The day we got back from New York, a Molly Ivins column appeared which called 34 Million Friends a splendid symbolic protest. Elation! Our first coverage by a nationally syndicated columnist. One of the best by golly.

Sign in Point G Hospital, Bamako, Mali

Chapter 6
UNFPA and SWOP and the MDGs

UNFPA came into being in 1969 at the behest of Richard Nixon who thought that knowledge of population trends and human numbers would be useful knowledge. Isn't it ironic that the nation responsible for UNFPA's founding has been its largest detractor during later Republican administrations? Today, UNFPA has morphed into both a research organization and a provider of reproductive health care services worldwide. Every year UNFPA puts out a State of World Population report called SWOP, the title for which in 2001 was "Footprints and Milestones: Population and Environmental Change." In several chapters, the vulnerability of women to pesticides, unclean water, and chemicals was highlighted. In 2002, the theme was population and poverty. It introduced the concept of a "demographic window" in poverty stricken countries when birth rates begin to fall and therefore there are, for the first time, significant numbers of adults who can be economically productive. Increased resources for economic development also become available.

What I love about these reports is that in the back there are tables. Every country is listed along with its present population, the expected population in 50 years, the total fertility rate

(TFR), the percentage of students who go to elementary and/or secondary school, the per capita income, the percentage of women who give birth with a trained attendant, and the percentage of the population with access to safe water. One could get a very good picture of the world if one were to take in all the information contained in a SWOP. In 2002, Lois and I took part in the press briefing at the National Press Club when UNFPA presented the 2002 report to the world. After the UNFPA experts presented their case and Lois and I had said our two minutes worth, I got up the nerve to put in my two cents worth to a reporter's question saying something like the Bush administration's "holier than thou" policies were shameful. That evening I caught a glimpse of Lois and me on the rerun on C-SPAN2. ... What, me on C-Span? Never in my wildest dreams!

"Making 1 Billion Count: Investing in Adolescents' Health and Rights" was the title of the 2003 SWOP. One of every five and a half people today on the planet is between the ages of 10 and 19, that's where the billion comes from. This is what is called a *youth bulge* and it exists particularly in poor countries. That is why a world population of 9 billion is predicted for 2050. About half the population of Iraq is under the age of 17. These young people need education and to have choices about their own families and jobs and they must have some hope for their futures. Knowing about AIDS and avoiding it would be nice too! This is a long term issue and should be at the top of the world's agenda.

The 2004 SWOP was "The Cairo Consensus at Ten: Population, Reproductive Health and the Global Effort to End Poverty." In 1994 in Cairo, Egypt, at the International Conference on Population and Development (ICPD), 179 countries including our own adopted a 20 year Programme of Action often called the Cairo Consensus. The year 2004 marked the halfway point of Cairo and the SWOP took stock of progress made and the long way still to go.

If over a twenty year period all children on the planet were to receive primary education. Of the illiterate people on the planet today, two-thirds of them are girls. Women who can read have a lower birth rate. It's almost as if the ability to read serves as a contraceptive. Girls who can read develop into women who play more active roles in their communities and economies. Female literacy is the key to opening doors for girls. It's really that simple.

I do want to quote this 2004 SWOP which quotes the ICPD Programme of Action on Reproductive Rights:

> "Reproductive rights embrace certain human rights that are already recognized in national laws, human rights documents and other consensus documents. These rights rest on the recognition of the basic right of all couples and individuals to decide freely and responsibly the number, spacing, and timing of their children and to have the information and means to do so, and the right to attain the highest standard of sexual and reproductive health. It also includes their right to make decisions concerning reproduction free of discrimination, coercion and violence, as expressed in human rights documents. In the exercise of this right, they should take into account the needs of their living and future children and their responsibilities towards the community. The promotion of the responsible exercise of these rights for all people should be the fundamental basis for government and community supported policies and programmes in the area of reproductive health, including family planning."

UNFPA in the 2004 SWOP states that 350 million couples still lack access to a full range of family planning services. Some 137 million women want to delay their next birth or avoid another, but are not using family planning. Services are reaching many more women than ever before, but are not expanding fast enough to close existing gaps or to keep pace with population growth and rising demand. Demand for family planning services will increase by 40 percent by 2025. Ouch!

What about abortion at Cairo? Essentially, there was a compromise. Abortion was never to be promoted as a method of family planning. "Improved access to family planning should help women avoid abortion, that those women who have recourse to abortion need humane treatment and need to have access to quality post-abortion care. Abortion policy, governments agreed, is a matter for national decision-making. Where abortion is not against the law, it should be safe."

My view, and I speak for myself only, is that with 40 women per minute seeking unsafe abortions around the world, mostly because they don't have access to reproductive health care and family planning, policies should change. Women often consider abortion a method of family planning! And then this wonderful world gives them post-abortion care for the hemorrhages and raging infections they suffer. But I also say that if the Cairo Consensus received full funding and implementation, the number of abortions could decrease dramatically. The fact that clandestine abortions are rampant shows utter contempt for the lives and full humanity of the female sex. I want to scream.

The Cairo Consensus also called for reducing infant, child, and maternal mortality. Progress is being made but too slowly. In the developing world, one third of all pregnant women receive no health care during pregnancy; sixty per cent of deliveries take place outside of health facilities; and skilled personnel assist only half of all deliveries. These are real people just like you and me. Imagine, as I did, yourself in this situation.

The world estimated that achieving Cairo by 2015 would necessitate between $17 and $20 billion per year. The target countries were to furnish about two-thirds of this amount, the developed world one-third. Broken promises all around, but the target countries have done much better than the developed world, which has come up with less than half of what it promised. The US is at the bottom. We were supposed to be furnishing about $1 billion a year by now. I think we're down to about $425 million.

And of course, with the AIDS epidemic swallowing up so many resources and with an average of 14,000 new infections per day, there is more need than ever for reproductive health care and education, especially among adolescents.

What is really galling is that money for AIDS has been separated from programs for reproductive health care and family planning. As if it would make sense to have an AIDS prevention program *over here* and a reproductive health care clinic *over there*. Really! Come on!

Have you ever heard of the UN's Millennium Development Goals known as the MDGs? Well, they are a blueprint for cutting world poverty by half by the year 2015. It is important to have goals against which you can measure progress, but one becomes a bit cynical when there is great fanfare about goals (such as at Cairo) and inadequate follow-through. Here are the MDGs.

1. **ERADICATE EXTREME POVERTY AND HUNGER.**
    By 2015, halve the proportion of people living on less than a dollar a day and those who suffer from hunger.

2. **ACHIEVE UNIVERSAL PRIMARY EDUCATION.**
    By 2015, ensure that all boys and girls complete primary school.f

3. **PROMOTE GENDER EQUALITY AND EMPOWER WOMEN.**
    Eliminate gender disparities in primary and secondary education preferably by 2005 and at all levels by 2015.

4.REDUCE CHILD MORTALITY.
    By 2015, reduce by two thirds the mortality rate of children under five.

5. **IMPROVE MATERNAL HEALTH.**
    By 2015, reduce by three quarters the ratio of women dying in childbirth.

6. **COMBAT HIV/AIDS, MALARIA AND OTHER DISEASES.**
    By 2015, halt and begin to reverse the spread of HIV/AIDS and the incidence of malaria and other major diseases.

7. **ENSURE ENVIRONMENTAL SUSTAINABILTIY.**
Integrate the principles of sustainable development into country policies and programmes and reverse the loss of environmental resources. By 2015, reduce by half the proportion of people without access to safe drinking water. By 2020, achieve significant improvement in the lives of at least 100 million slum dwellers.s

8. **DEVELOP A GLOBAL PARTNERSHIP FOR DEVELOPMENT.**
Develop further an open trading and financial system that includes a commitment to good governance, development and poverty reduction nationally and internationally. Address the least-developed countries' special needs, and the special needs of landlocked and small island developing states. Deal comprehensively with developing countries' debt problems. Develop productive work for youth. In cooperation with pharmaceutical companies, provide access to affordable essential drugs in developing countries. In cooperation with the private sector, make available the benefits of new technologies, especially information and communications technologies.

In many ways you can see that the goals and targets set at the Cairo ICPD anticipated the MDGs. But the Cairo goal of universal access to quality reproductive health services (which certainly includes family planning!) by 2015 is not one of the MDGs. My own opinion, speaking for myself, is that the world weaseled again.

I will, though, quote Kofi Annan at the Fifth Asian and Pacific Population Conference, held in Bangkok in December 2002. "The Millennium Development Goals, particularly the eradication of extreme poverty and hunger, cannot be achieved if questions of population and reproductive health are not squarely addressed. And that means stronger efforts to promote women's rights, and greater investment in education and health, including reproductive health and family planning."

At least he used the FP (family planning) word! Every day I read about empowering women, empowering girls, supporting women, supporting girls, saving women's lives and on and on and on and the FP word is not used.

I think that the reason is in part, maybe even in large part, so as not to offend the "pro-life" Bush administration which in several international venues has voted against reaffirming the Cairo agreement. The US has stood alone in this. For instance, at Santiago, Chile, we were voted down 22 to 1. My opinion is that the Bush administration is, not so subtly, even against FP. UNFPA, which I remind you provides family planning and no abortions, estimates that $34 million would prevent 800,000 abortions. Go figure!

Above: Lives saved by c-sections in a clinic with UNFPA trained doctor, Tambacounda Province, Senegal, Below: This couple wanted to be treated for infertility,

Chapter 7
Senegal, Mali, Nicaragua, East Timor
(www.endfistula.org)

By December 2002, UNFPA could see that envelopes were piling up. I think that they were rather amazed, and they asked Lois and me if we would like to see their work on site. They knew by now that we were two pretty serious people. When we met UNFPA officials for the first time back in October, they had asked us how we saw this effort, how serious we were. Lois said she was in until we got our $34 million and my exact words were "All the way forever" because quite honestly this is it for me. For me it's a *vision* thing. (It is for Lois too, but she is also an attorney involved in technology arbitration cases, grows grapes in Australia and is a grandmother of seven!) I said right away that I would like to go to Senegal because I had some Senegalese friends and I also speak fluent French. UNFPA decided that I should also go to Mali. Lois chose Nicaragua and later she went to East Timor (Timor Leste).

Here are the records of our trips. I do hope that after you read these accounts, that you will have a good concept of what reproductive health care is all about. I hope you think that the two hundredths of one percent of our federal budget we allot for this is grossly inadequate. Anything spent in this area is for the long term. It has long term beneficial results not only for the people and countries it helps, but for America's reputation in the world.

My Senegal/Mali trip

I went to New York on January 30, 2003 and on the 31st was briefed by Espérance Fundira, program specialist for Africa from UNFPA. She had been in the field for nine years. I then met Cheryl from the US Committee who had arranged an interview with Mae Cheng of Newsday. We had about a half hour interview. I remember putting my hand on Mae's shoulder and saying, "The American people deserve to know about this effort."

That evening the UNFPA held its holiday party about a month late but unbelievably they seem to have waited for me. The staff at UNFPA comes from all over the world. I said to all the people gathered that the American people say hello, that the American people will be represented in the work of UNFPA, and I thanked them for supporting us and welcoming our efforts from the very beginning. And then we all ate like pigs and I danced the jitterbug with Thoraya.

Our plane left late that night. Our flight being delayed, we had a chance for a snack of fruit and crackers and Roquefort cheese. There was a young guy reading Le Monde and he turned out to be Todd Berault an employee of Pfizer Pharmaceuticals with a degree in business from Columbia. He promised to raise $100 from his friends for 34 Million Friends.

Our Air France flight from Paris to Dakar, Senegal was delayed by an ice storm so we waited for 5 hours in the airport and then 3 hours on the plane. They, at least, served us a 4 course dinner. We arrived in Dakar at 1:00 a.m. and were whisked to the

Ambassador Hall at the airport itself. Senegalese TV interviewed me there.

I explained that Bush's action was really a crime against humanity and that the American people were stretching out a hand of friendship. We left the airport at 3:00 a.m. and took a taxi to the Afifa hotel. On one side of the road there were sheep grazing, because February 13 was a religious holiday when all families slaughter and eat a sheep. The rolling Atlantic was on the other side of the road.

I got to bed at 3:30 and slept until 9:15, took an OJ from my in-room refrigerator and wrote in my diary. Mari Tikkanen, the Finnish woman accompanying me on the trip, Alvaro Serrano from Media Services at UNFPA, and I had a breakfast of bread, butter, *confiture de fraises*, 2 yoghurts and good coffee out by the pool. Mari's room had no hot water and she heard disco music all night so when we got back to Dakar after our 9 days, we did stay in a better place. After breakfast we went to the UNFPA headquarters in Dakar where we met the whole crowd going on the trip and took some pictures. I think the government officials, UNFPA people, and I took up 4 land cruisers, but I will tell you this: Sturdy vehicles are necessary because of the quality of the roads. We drove for seven and one half hours to the Tambacounda province which is almost to the Mali border.

This was my first time ever in Africa. On the road we saw monkeys, snakes, giraffes, pelicans, hyenas and a few lions. I marveled at the baobab trees because of my intimate knowledge of Saint-Exupéry's **The Little Prince**. I learned that seventy-five percent of the elementary schools in Senegal are for both boys and girls and that there is a division between the French schools which are more like ours and the religious schools which are based on teaching the Koran.

My impression during the drive was that there were people, and children particularly, everywhere, especially leaving Dakar. I have never seen so many people, and so much stuff.

Truthfully, it all looked rather chaotic. It was my first impression of a very poor country. We stopped for lunch in a café where there was a big anti-AIDS poster on the wall. I talked to the representative of the Ministère des Finances about 34 Million Friends and to Ismael, the acting head of the UNFPA mission in Senegal about polygamy, schooling, religion, and female genital mutilation (FGM). We drove until 7:30 p.m. Our hotel was Le Relai de Tambacounda where there was a swimming pool and air conditioning. I gratefully drank a Fanta Orange in the lobby. We all had a good chicken dinner. Before bed, I showered and washed my hair. Tomorrow would be a big day.

When you go into a district you must call on the Governor. The next morning we were ushered into the headquarters and had quite a formal session where the governor, dressed in white, welcomed us and said that he hoped we would find many more than 34 million friends. It was obvious that he greatly appreciated the work of UNFPA in his district. And he seemed to have real understanding of the importance of tending to women's needs.

We then drove one more hour to a village which was, to put it mildly, *way out there* in the no-road bush. At this village the people gathered and danced for us, and then there was a ceremony where I awarded diplomas to the Community Based Health Workers on which much of UNFPA's system is based. UNFPA can't be everywhere so they train people in first aid, two-way communication, in reproductive health, and they give them supplies to use and then hopefully there is a clinic within reach for emergencies. Our next visit was to just such a clinic.

The clinic has changed the whole life of the community. First of course we met the imam. Then we talked to the doctors, the anesthetist, and to the several midwives. We saw the delivery room (Mari saw a baby being born) and I visited with two women whose lives had been saved by c-sections. A picture of one of them, Sissoko, was subsequently featured on the home page of the UNFPA web site. I then sat next to a woman who had just given birth to her 4th child at age 22. She was anemic, as was the baby. The clinic was going to make a real effort at offering the couple family planning and treatment for the anemia. On the walls of the clinic there were signs saying: *"Bébé, avec les seins, tu seras sain."* In French this rhymes and it says, "Baby, with breast-feeding, you will be healthy." I went to the bathroom and found no toilet paper. They have little pots of water instead which you pour over yourself. Hmmm, I prefer good old American toilet paper.

At one of the joint UNFPA-government health centers I met what you'd call in French a *griot*, a kind of wandering minstrel who sings songs in tribal languages in the various villages against female genital mutilation, against very early marriage, against promiscuity and behavior that might lead to HIV. A wonderful way to educate people, many of whom don't read.

Then away we went to an elementary school which is funded by the government of Senegal and UNFPA. The children are taught to read and write. The classes are taught in French, not in a tribal language. A big part of the curriculum is Family Life Education. After a welcoming ceremony and my being welcomed by the kids, who held up signs reading "Welcome Mrs. Jane Roberts and her 34 Million Friends," I visited a classroom where the children put on a skit warning against "fooling around," against early marriage, and early pregnancy (*grossesse précoce*). Here I picked up a children's writing booklet on the front of which are the seals of the Ministry of Education of Senegal and of the UNFPA and where it says in big letters: "Little girls have as much right to food, education, and health care as little boys." That this message needs to be said speaks volumes but that UNFPA is saying it shows the down to earth wonderful educational role it tries to fulfill. The US isn't funding this?

At the school, I also met with the parents' committee (PTA) and told them that I lived next to an elementary school in my home town and that for several years I had gone over and tutored reading as a volunteer. I congratulated them for being volunteers for their school. I have the welcome sign the kids made for me here at home.

Then it was on to a high school where they had an Internet connection and had downloaded a press conference on 34 Million Friends. The main subject of this high school was the environment. They had gardens and grew food and dug wells for clean water.

On we went to a junior high school where I presented a television, a gift from UNFPA, for their educational program. In the evening there was a village meeting outside, where a big screen was mounted. A video in the Wolof language about the dangers of early pregnancy was shown, followed by a long village discussion that lasted until dark. I sat next to the UNFPA program director and asked a million questions, one of which was: "In America, often a young couple gets married and both the wife and husband work for several years while using family planning. Does that ever happen here?" "No," he said, "that would not be part of the culture."

We got back to the hotel at 7:45 p.m. We had left at 8:30 a.m. and had had no lunch. Two impressions I got were that much is based on ceremony, which is important, and there is a very strong group dynamic and togetherness in Senegalese life.

The next day we visited the Tambacounda regional health center. There were perhaps 100 pregnant women waiting for appointments. Another skit was enacted about the need for prenatal care. I said that I was going to speak about this clinic back in the United States and that I was going to try to *sensibiliser les Américains* to the facts of the high maternal and infant death rates in Senegal.

At the clinic that day was a young woman who had come 9 kilometers on horseback to try to find out why she wasn't getting pregnant for a second time. She and her husband were devastated. Unfortunately, her pregnancy test was negative. UNFPA and the Senegalese health center are not only interested in family planning and contraception. Their emphasis is on human rights and individual choice. The clinic was going to try to help this woman conceive.

We then drove back to Dakar for a press conference the next morning. This was unbelievable. There were at least 30 journalists, and radio and TV reporters—a roomful to say the least. After introductions and remarks by government officials and UNFPA representatives, it was my turn. My innermost thoughts were "Oh my gosh, here I am, speaking to a whole country, in French no less, Jane, for God's sakes, don't blow it!" I had written down my first sentence just to make sure I could get started. *"Je tiens à vous remercier de l'accueil chaleureux que vous les Sénégalais m'avez fait."* (I really want to thank all of the Senegalese people for the warm welcome you have given me.) I then told them all I had observed during my days there. I explained that many Americans found the Bush Administration incomprehensible. I said that I had been profoundly disappointed by this decision and had come up with a brainstorm of asking 34 million Americans to give one dollar. And I said that another woman, Lois Abraham, had had exactly the same idea and that this had become *Les 34 Millions d'Amis*, that 2000 envelopes were arriving per day and that we were very close to having collected $500,000, going up by about $10,000 per day.

I said there seemed to be wonderful cooperation between their government, UNFPA and other NGO's working in the field of reproductive health. In the long run it was probably the most important work on earth and that it ought to be one the world's first priorities. I said I would tell Americans all about my visit and I extended a hand of friendship from the American people, who were not being well represented by their government.

After the formal press conference broke up, I had several private interviews with radio and TV reporters and learned that this received big play in *Le Soleil*, their main newspaper and on French speaking TV. ... Never in my wildest dreams!

After the press conference, we went to Le Dantec, the main hospital in Dakar. We had a session with Dr. Jean Charles Moreau and other doctors who said they lacked paramedics, surgical supplies, incubators and family planning commodities. Morale, they said, was very low. These doctors were being honest. In the gynecology and obstetric clinic at the hospital, at least one hundred women were awaiting their appointments. Many looked tired and discouraged. One room was reserved for Natural Family Planning and a nurse was explaining the "take your temperature" method to a patient. It's a choice I keep telling myself, but yuck. There are too many premature births, neo-natal infections and deaths. I can't choose for others, but I say if a woman doesn't want to get pregnant, or is not healthy enough to sustain a healthy pregnancy, I'd like to see her use what most of us in the US use, the pill, or an IUD, or Depo Provera, or Norplant or something SURE. Natural family planning, which is based on abstinence at certain periods, is not a sure fire method and often the woman has not the *power* to enforce the rules. Of course I might have been misreading the situation, and this woman might have been learning her fertile periods by temperature in order to conceive. So shame on me!

We caught a 4:00 a.m. flight on Cameroon Airlines from Dakar to Bamako, Mali and went to our hotel, Le Diplomate, very near the UN offices and the center of town. Our first visit later that morning was to the Centre Communautaire de Sabalibougou. This is a very poor area in a very poor city, in a very poor country, one of the 10 poorest countries in the world. The total fertility rate is over 7 children per woman and there are high infant and maternal death rates. This "centre" represents woman power. The women of the neighborhood, realizing their desperate need for a reproductive health care clinic, started a garbage and trash recycling business, made a little seed money, and went to their government and to UNFPA. The result is a wonderful clinic where I saw many women coming to get their children vaccinated.

The doctor actually lives on the grounds to be there at all times. There were women in labor, women coming for family planning. However, the clinic was lacking in laboratory facilities, something we would find appalling. I met an "older" wife with 8 kids who brings the "younger wives" for family planning!

We returned to UNFPA headquarters for lunch with about 30 government and UNFPA leaders. That afternoon was a high and a low, because I learned so much about what shouldn't even exist in the 21st century, OBSTETRIC FISTULA. Now you know what it is. Now you know that with this rip in the birth canal that women can drip urine and feces from the "wrong hole". Imagine living with this!

We went to the Point G hospital which is the main hospital in Bamako, the capital of Mali. The Urology Department is where Dr. Kalilou Ouattara does the obstetric fistula repair operations. On the grounds of the Point G hospital is the OASIS where about 40 women who are suffering from fistula live. They told me their stories. One story was among the saddest I have every heard. Twenty-two year old Sissoko after a long labor had a dead baby come out along with urine signifying a fistula. Her husband chased her out and she returned to her parents and found a second man who accepted her as his wife. She again became pregnant and this time actually went to her rural hospital thinking that they would know what to do. The hospital left her in labor for 4 days and she ended up with a rectal fistula and so much scar tissue that she had to have a major section of her colon removed. Other women also had stories. They live there, support themselves with crafts, sometimes are visited by their families and they wait for their surgeries. —Early in 2004, I received word that a whole new operating room paid for by 34 Million Friends is up and running and Dr. Ouattara is thrilled.

Just a bit more. UNFPA is really making strides with their Fistula Campaign. On July 26, 2005, Lois and I were briefed on their worldwide approach. Being as the sufferers are usually the most marginalized girls and women, and that these women are part of UNFPA's mandate from the world community, UNFPA is proceeding with needs assessments in 21 countries. A needs assessment is basically an educated guess based on extensive surveys about the extent of the problem. Prevention is of course the key, but if a fistula develops, treatment, i.e. surgery, and then reintegration into the community are key for the psycho-social well being of the patient. UNFPA recently hosted a Fistula Fortnight in Nigeria where over a two week period, doctors and care-givers were trained and 545 women underwent surgery. A modern new fistula facility in Angola is in the works.

Nathalie Imbruglia, whose picture graces L'Oréal cosmetics ads, has adopted fistula as her cause. Engel Entertainment will soon be putting out a film called "A Walk to Beautiful" for all to see. And nothing is more fitting than that title because when a young girl or woman is cured of her fistula, she can again walk out of the shadows into the sunlight of life.

Later that afternoon, we were off to a Youth Center which combines a soccer field, youth counseling, and a health facility. The idea is to attract the young with sports and then have them learn about the other available services. Lots of HIV/AIDS education goes on there. I met with a whole group of peer counselors who reach out to the young.

The next day we were on the road again toward the village of Markacoungo. A very poor road and it seemed to me that it was filled with donkey carts and broken down flat-tired trucks piled high with belongings. Again, I was greeted by the mayor of the village but, because we were late, he was told that we couldn't make the planned visit of his school. He grabbed me by the hand anyway and led me to the 3 year old village school which started out with 500 students and now has 1000 and it is funded by UNFPA. He wore a Mali flag over his shoulder. Such pride! This was a coed school, girls and boys!

In another district, we made our introductory call on the High Commissioner who was lamenting the amount spent on arms in the world when his people needed health care. I shook my head and said, "*Oh, ne m'en parlez pas!*" (You don't have to tell me!). We then drove 90 kilometers to the village of Bla, to a UNFPA clinic which serves 9 villages. This clinic has two operating rooms and is staffed 24/7 by doctors and midwives.

The clinic is at the end of the paved road and off we went on a dirt road toward the village of Nyamana. Six miles out we came upon *my* woman lying on the donkey cart, in labor, struggling to reach the clinic to give birth. The doctor who was with us loaded her on the back of his truck and a midwife climbed aboard and off they went, back to the clinic. The Woman on the Donkey Cart is my symbol for this entire effort. I asked her if I could take her picture and use it to show around the world to benefit UNFPA. A shy woman, she finally said yes and I have kept my promise in many ways, in my talks, in the slides I show, and in the poem I wrote, and in the picture in this book.

The village of Nyamana for several years has had the benefit of community based health workers trained by UNFPA and of the clinic which is within reach. The whole village came out to tell me how the health of women and children had improved, how fewer women and children were dying, and they were very open about sharing the types of family planning they used. Of course, they spoke in a tribal language, bambara, and then this was translated into French for me. I met several of the community based health workers, one a young man who had been given micro-credit to have a little store. I took a photo of him holding up a box of condoms. A young wife had been given micro-credit to raise sheep. It was here that I had the thought of feeling like Princess Diana must have felt, with so many people wanting to tell me their stories. We then drove back to Bamako.

The press conference at the Maison de la Presse took place on Saturday, February 8 in Bamako. There was again a roomful of journalists. Looking at my notes, this is what I said: I thanked them for their welcome. I spoke of my very long interest in the subject of reproductive health. I shared the fact that so many people had told me their stories, which I said reflects the high degree of cooperation between UNFPA, the government, and other NGO's working in the field of reproductive health. I added very sincerely that I was in awe at the devotion of the service providers and at the gratitude of the people served. I said that this was really the most important cause on earth, that it should come first in world priorities and that I would speak about the people of Mali and Senegal when I returned home.

After the press conference, I had a long meeting with women leaders of Mali at the ASDAP headquarters. ASDAP stands for Association de Soutien au Développement des Activités de Population (Association of Support for the Development of Population Activities). These women were fighters and completely dedicated. There is a cyber café at ASDAP, all the computers were in use by the young, but one of them looked up www.unfpa.org for me and it was on this day, at that time, that I learned that 34 Million Friends had surpassed $500,000. We then went to a very nice restaurant for a very "European" lunch, then back to the hotel to pack.

Before leaving Africa, I want to say a few words about Dr. Miriam Cissoko who accompanied us the entire time we were in Mali and about Younes Zoughlami, a Tunisian who is the head of the UNFPA mission in Mali. Miriam practiced her English with me. She spoke quite well. And her dedication to and love for the fistula patients was something to behold. Younes Zoughlami and I had several long philosophical discussions about the meaning of life and the injustices of the world. In early April 2004, I received a lengthy email from him describing the wonderful way our 34 Million Friends money had furnished a whole new operating room in the Urology Department for the fistula surgeries.

Back in New York on Sunday, February 9, I know I took a walk to the Pong Sri restaurant again and nearly didn't make it back to the hotel because of "intestinal problems". Was it a change in diet or Air France? Luckily, I had planned ahead and had medication. On Monday and Tuesday, I told UNFPA people and US Committee people all about the trip. I learned so much. I wish you could have come with me.

Lois' Story

Nicaragua, February19-20, 2003

"It is much more important to have a friend than a dollar." That excellent sound bite came from the Nicaraguan Country Representative of UNFPA, Tomas Jimenez, during a discussion of 34 Million Friends. Tomas heads the cooperation program in Nicaragua, and like every UNFPA representative I have met, he is intelligent, dedicated, and effective in communicating UNFPA's commitment to working in partnership with governments to promote a human rights based approach to reproductive health. Tomas acknowledges that the dollars are important too: Without dollars, there are no programs.

UNFPA invited me to visit some programs in Nicaragua so I could report back to you how UNFPA focuses its efforts and invests its (your) money. In two days my brain and heart were assaulted with information and images that will never leave me.

First, some background. Nicaragua is a beautiful but strained country with beautiful but strained people. The last century brought Nicaragua years of political instability, civil war, a horrendous earthquake, and hurricane Mitch.

Nicaragua has one of the highest population growth rates in Latin America, one of the highest fertility rates, one of the highest teenage pregnancy rates and one of the highest maternal mortality rates. There is also a high rate of unmet demand for modern contraceptive methods, and, as a result, sterilization is a default contraception method. There is a lot of work to be done. With all that said, Nicaraguans are anything but beaten. They are energetically and creatively determined to control the forces they can control and be prepared for those they cannot.

Second, some of the programs: (In selecting these, I am leaving out equally important and effective ones.) I'll start in a place that may surprise some of you—our visit to the Sergeant's School of the National Army. The commander of the school, a Lieutenant Colonel, knew exactly what he wanted: healthy soldiers. So, part of the training curriculum for the sergeants is a very frank, very comprehensive course in reproductive health and reproductive rights. As the Colonel said, men who are embarrassed to talk about issues of sex and reproductive health openly, will, if they become sick, try to hide their illness and illness will spread.

The Colonel sees his responsibility for education in concentric circles, starting with his circle of soldiers, spreading to a circle of their families, and finally to the communities around them. The school trains about 2,000 men each year. The colonel's program seems to be working; sexually transmitted disease has been limited to four cases in each of the past two years.

Another group we visited was working at the policy level—three women elected to Parliament, all members of the Sandinista political party. Women fought alongside men in the civil war, and that changed their position in society. One of the most respected individuals in the country is Violetta Chamorro, who in 1990 won the presidency in the first democratically held election in six decades. The three women who met with us held the equivalent positions of committee chairs in our House or Senate. They discussed their initiatives for empowerment of women, equal opportunity, reduction of family violence, and reproductive health. They are sponsoring legislation on family law and equal rights. They are impressive and tough!

I have saved the worst and best for last. We traveled inland to Matagalpa, a coffee growing center once reasonably prosperous but now impoverished due to the collapsed coffee market. Some growers are not even bothering to harvest their beans. The result is no work. Children are suffering from malnutrition.

In Matagalpa we visited the Casa Materna, which provides free care for near-term pregnant women who are at risk because they are too young or too old, already have had many pregnancies (the record is 24), or because they live in such isolated areas that if they need help in labor they would be unable to get it because of lack of transportation. After delivery, the Casa takes care of them for at least eight days or until they are strong enough to return to their homes. They are also given family planning information and contraceptives if they want them.

The Casa is equipped for 20 women, but because they never turn away anyone at risk, capacity is sometimes extended to 40, and the women share the available beds. The women pay nothing. Their level of poverty is so profound that even the most modest charge would make it impossible for them to come to the Casa.

The highly-respected senora who runs the Casa shared her story with me. After marrying, she lived in isolation on a coffee plantation. She delivered eight babies alone, cutting the umbilical cord herself. Her husband was never present for a birth and no one else lived close by. She went to her mother and told her that she was afraid of being so isolated, but her mother responded that her place was with her husband. So she returned to the plantation and had more babies. She says, "I am not like that now!" and I believe her!

We also spoke to Elsa, a 23 year-old who was having her third child at the Casa. She had managed to get to the fourth grade and wanted to continue, but her family was too poor; she had to leave school to work. After she married, her husband raised subsistence food for them when he no longer had work in the coffee *fincas*. She wanted to work, but knew there was none available. Her dream was to see her children educated.

UNFPA has been able to partner with a variety of efforts in Nicaragua to improve the quality of lives and in particular women's lives. Words are inadequate to describe the spirit of the Nicaraguan people and the challenges they face. I wish everyone could have this face-to-face experience. The world would work better.

Lois in Timor Leste (East Timor), October 2003

Jane Roberts and I started 34 Million Friends because we believe that our government's action in withholding funds from UNFPA is brutally harmful to women and children in countries where even small acts of generosity can prevent needless deaths. The loss of the promised $34 million left a 12% hole in the UNFPA budget for projects that save women's lives around the world.

Timor Leste (East Timor) was a beneficiary of part of the first $1 million raised by 34 Million Friends. UNFPA's work in Timor Leste shows not only how great the need for UNFPA is, but also how very effective the organization is in working from a human rights base within local communities.

The plight of Timor Leste and its courageous people no longer commands world attention. It has been pushed out of the headlines by the campaign against terrorism and the war in Iraq, but the East Timorese, like the Iraqis, have suffered unspeakable brutality and like the Iraqis, they are trying to establish a functioning state to take the place of a repressive regime.

After nearly 175 years of colonialism, first under the Portuguese for 150 years, then under the Indonesians from 1975 until 1995, The East Timorese voted for an independent state. Their Indonesian occupiers left, but systematically destroyed the country's infrastructure, slashing, burning, and raping their way out. Now the East Timorese, with the help of the United Nations and many governmental and non-governmental organizations, are trying to build a democratic state.

UNFPA helps the East Timorese address one of the most acute problems, a shortage of basic medical services for women and their families. All statistics about East Timor are estimates since no one knows exactly how many people have survived the years of violence and turmoil. The best estimate of the fertility rate is 7.4, which means each woman has an average of 7.4 pregnancies. The maternal mortality rate is somewhere between 600 and 800 per 100,000. Either number is shockingly high. Diarrhea is a major cause of death among infants and toddlers. Difficult economic times and a lack of employment have also fostered a high rate of another serious risk to women and children: domestic violence. UNFPA works with the fledgling government and local relief organizations, as well as other NGOs with efforts in Timor Leste, to alleviate these life and death problems.

Four doctors trained in obstetrics and gynecology serve the entire population of Timor Leste. The population is estimated at between 800,000 and 900,000. Next July, a UNFPA-sponsored census will be taken and the actual numbers determined. The doctors have all been recruited by UNFPA, their salaries are paid by UNFPA, and they are all saving women's lives every day.

Three of the doctors staff the maternity facilities at the National Hospital Guido Valadares, one of the few institutions left standing in Dili, the East Timor capital after the Indonesians left. Dr. Sevinj, a beautiful woman from Azerbaijan, and Dr. Marisa, an equally beautiful woman from the Philippines, were tempted into working for UNFPA in Timor Leste because of the range of experiences such a posting offers a young doctor. In that regard, they have not been disappointed. Up to 30 deliveries a day at the hospital, many of them complicated deliveries, have honed their skills. Dr. Majiec worked with the UN in Kosovo. He is experienced in the stresses of providing medical care under difficult conditions.

We visited the hospital to see the doctors in action. Our agenda notation seemed straightforward enough:

Visit National Hospital
Meet with doctors and visit Maternity Room
Visit Safe Room.

Our US-based assumptions of what "visit Maternity Room" means were almost immediately confounded. The various maternity rooms were large, multi-bedded, airy, and clean. One was assigned to women in labor, another to women and their infants post-delivery. No one complains about the hospital food because there is none. Instead, the patients' families bring food. Often that means that entire families come to the hospital, and the maternity rooms had something of the look of very clean bus stations with beds. Men, women, and children carrying bundles were everywhere.

"Meet with doctors" on the agenda gave no hint that we would meet them in the operating room—not the high tech stainless steel room of our mental images, though scrubbed clean—and view first hand and close up an emergency c-section. (The patient was fully awake and after being informed that there were visitors who supported the medical program, she was positive in giving consent to our presence.)

The confidence and competence of the doctors was obvious and reassuring. Everyone in the operating room celebrated with the mother at the successful delivery of a very big baby boy, too big for a normal delivery from the slight East Timorese woman lying exhausted but elated on the delivery table.

Finally, we visited the Safe Room. The Safe Room, another UNFPA-supported project, has been established at the Hospital as temporary shelter for victims of family violence.

The phrase "family violence" has become a familiar one—abstract, almost, in its impact. The reality is anything but abstract, as we discovered that morning. We were viewing the pleasant, quiet room when the Sister in charge that day entered and said something urgent to our guide. He immediately led us out to the room and down the hall past two policemen and a man holding a beautiful curly-haired little girl who was clinging to him with both arms wrapped around his neck. We learned a few moments later that the child had been raped by her uncle. Her father had carried her to the Safe Room.

The women and babies in the Maternity Rooms and the child in the Safe Room are destined to lead difficult and dangerous lives in Timor Leste. They will not escape the perils of living in a poor, struggling country. They will be at risk from malaria or dengue fever with every mosquito bite. But at least in times of immediate need, they have a place to go where they can get trained, compassionate care. UNFPA is there to help them.

We, the U.S, should be there to help UNFPA. You are invited to help through 34 Million Friends of UNFPA.

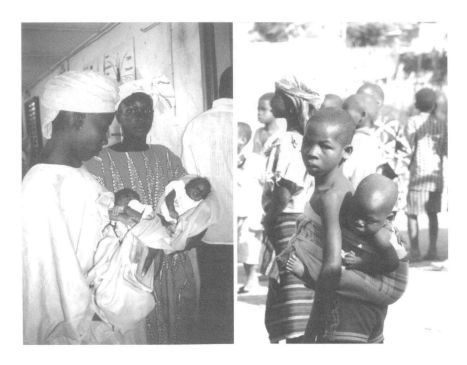

Left: Women waiting for vaccinations for their babies at UNFPA sponsored clinic .
Right: Girls take care of younger children

Chapter 8
Our First Million Dollars

I mentioned Molly Ivins' column. Sometime in early December 2002, Molly Ivins had lunch with Ellen Goodman of the *Boston Globe* in Boston and mentioned 34 Million Friends to her. Ellen had previously written a column that called the Bush decision mind-boggling. So, in mid-December Ellen called both Lois and me and wrote a column which appeared on December 22, of 2002.

I want to reprint Ellen's column here because it is vintage Goodman. She tells the truth.

Friendly Dollars
by Ellen Goodman

"AT FIRST the letters just trickled in to the United Nations Population Fund. A dollar here, five dollars there. It was enough to buy a few birthing kits or cure a 14-year old mother of the silent plague of fistula.

Of course it didn't begin to make up for the $34 million that the Bush Administration denied the international family planning group. But the trickle didn't stop either. It grew all fall until an astonished woman at the UNFPA decided to invest in an electronic letter opener.

Now, it's beginning to look a lot like Christmas. Every day, 500 or 600 more letters arrive in the New York office from Americans bearing gifts to women overseas. Some include a dollar for every member of the family or for everyone in the office or in the church.

The UNFPA's Mari Tikkanen, who stays after work with other volunteers to take the money out of the envelopes, stopping occasionally to read the letters to each other, says, "I've never seen anything like it." Maybe there hasn't been anything quite like it.

About six months ago, two women who had never met had the same thought. Jane Roberts, a retired French teacher, and Lois Abraham, a lawyer, were both outraged when Bush reneged on funds for the UNFPA. This was money for contraception and sex education, for maternal healthcare and AIDS education. It would have helped prevent 2 million unwanted pregnancies, 800,000 abortions, 4,700 maternal deaths.

Roberts wrote a letter to the editor of her local paper: "More women die in childbirth in a few days than terrorism kills people in a year. Ho hum. Some little girl is having her genitals cut with a cactus needle. Ho hum." Abraham, meanwhile, asked herself, "How come we aren't screaming from the rooftops?" She sent out an email calling family planning "a humanitarian issue, not a political one."

Independently, the two women came up with what Roberts called an "exercise in outraged democracy." What would happen, they asked, if 34 million Americans each gave a dollar to make up for the money?" So was born "34 Million Friends."

Does the campaign have an amateurish quality? Hey kids, we could do the show right here? So be it. Roberts says, "We want 34 million Americans to have their own teeny-tiny foreign policy." Maybe we all need one.

From the moment Bush was sworn into office, his administration sacrificed international family planning to the farthest tip of the right wing of his party. First came the global gag rule refusing funds to any group that would tell a woman where she could get an abortion, even in countries where abortion was legal. Next came a withholding of money to UNFPA on the blatantly false grounds that the organization helped the Chinese government push coercive abortions.

Despite all the hoo-ha about liberating Afghan women, the White House has never acknowledged that women's freedom includes the freedom to decide when and how to have children. The women in the poorest parts of the world were held hostage to domestic politics. Did the administration think we'd never notice? Never care?

It wasn't enough to withdraw family planning funds. At the recent, contentious U.N. population conference, our government went even further. It tried to overturn international agreements. Asian countries had come to Bangkok to implement the 1994 UN Cairo agreement on population. They wanted to talk about gender equality and poverty, contraception and HIV. The United States came to unravel the agreement. They wanted to talk about natural family planning and to delete any references to "reproductive health."

Among the US delegates was a man who previously represented the Vatican and a woman who lectured the Asians on her own success using the rhythm method. Our country ended up an isolated minority of one.

This administration is nostalgic for the days before women's rights. Is it any wonder that some Americans have responded to 34 Million Friends? This is an idea that comes with an address, a place where we can offer aid as well as dissent, a dollar as well as a message of connection to the women of the world.

It took months for the campaign to reach its first $100,000. It took just weeks to add in another $50,000. If the goal of $34 million sounds elusive, UNFPA's Tikkanen says, "When it hit $1000, I was thrilled. Now I don't think anything is impossible."

One dollar per person. Abraham calls it an "entry fee" to have your voice heard. I call it a pretty low price for a new, improved foreign policy."

With both Molly's and Ellen's columns, and an editorial in the *Capital Times* in Madison, Wisconsin, and an editorial in the *Atlanta Journal and Constitution* and our own outreach at which Lois and I were both spending long hours every day... well, to make a long story short, UNFPA and the US Committee were inundated with envelopes. Such that on May 1, 2003, we had our Million Dollar press conference at UNFPA headquarters in New York City.

The night before in my hotel, I had a phone interview with the *Chicago Tribune*. On the morning of the press conference, there was a wonderful display in the lobby of UNFPA with pictures of Lois and me, piles of envelopes, copies of letters people had written. I was thrilled to see reporters from the *Los Angeles Times*, from *Marie Claire*, the BBC, Edie Lederer who is the Associated Press reporter for the UN, CNN, and others. That same afternoon a reporter from the *New York Times* interviewed us and an article appeared with a picture. Not too many days after this press conference a friend from high school days saw me on CNN International in Malawi, but nothing appeared on CNN in this country.

After the press conference, during which Tim Wirth, President of the UN Foundation, announced that it was awarding a 25 cents on the dollar gift for the second million, we had an audio press conference with about 25 reporters signed up from around the country. A wonderful Chinese lunch followed, then a party for Alvaro Serrano who is the web person at UNFPA and who had visited both Lois and me in our homes to document our lives.

That evening Lois, her husband Dick, and I went out for a French dinner at La Caravelle. We paid $72 each for a prix fixe menu of smoked salmon, quenelles and crème brûlée. Not worth it money wise but we were definitely trying to support French restaurants because others, we heard, were boycotting them because of French opposition to the Iraq war. We three walked back to our hotel down 5th Avenue. What a day. Unbelievable for a retired French teacher and tennis coach! And it was also on this day that Lois and I met David and Ellen who would be helping us with 34 Million Friends for the next two years.

Let me insert here what our first million dollars paid for. This comes from our website.

$1,000,000 from Americans in Support of UNFPA

Over 100,000 Americans have voiced their support for international family planning through the "34 Million Friends of UNFPA" campaign. The first million dollars raised from the campaign will help make pregnancy and childbirth safer for women; reduce the spread of HIV/AIDS; equip hospitals with essential family planning supplies; support adolescents and youth, and prevent and treat obstetric fistula. Country-specific programmes include:

- In **Timor-Leste**, UNFPA will equip the only two hospitals in the country that provide emergency obstetric care with two-way radios to reach on-call doctors in time to save women's lives. In addition, three Timorese doctors will receive obstetrical training to ensure that women in need of Caesarean sections can get help outside the two main hospitals. Currently, the country relies heavily on expatriate doctors and there is an urgent need for local expertise. UNFPA will also provide 80 motorcycles to midwives to reach women living in districts with poor roads and no public transportation.

- In **Ghana**, UNFPA will purchase essential reproductive health equipment for clinics that provide safe motherhood services to young women and adolescent girls. This includes supplies to treat women who have suffered from female genital cutting.

- In **Rwanda**, UNFPA will provide ambulances to transfer patients in need of emergency obstetric care. Voluntary counselling and testing kits for HIV/AIDS will also be provided to health clinics. There is a high demand for testing thanks to community outreach campaigns. Therapy kits will also be provided to treat women who are victims of sexual abuse.

- In **Eritrea**, UNFPA will train 1,000 health assistants in basic emergency obstetric care in an effort to reduce the high incidence of maternal mortality. This training will teach providers how to perform life-saving interventions for complicated deliveries, thus "buying time" before a woman can reach a hospital. There are only a limited number of facilities that provide emergency obstetric care in the country.

- In **Mongolia**, UNFPA will provide information on modern contraceptive methods to adolescents, men and women nationwide. Most people rely on traditional methods and are unaware that modern contraceptive methods are available, affordable and reliable. Clinical guidelines on treatment of disease and illness during pregnancy will also be distributed to all reproductive health service providers. In addition, 63 health care providers from the country's 21 provinces will be taught how to provide quality reproductive health care and counselling. Skilled providers are particularly needed in remote rural areas.

- In **Bhutan**, UNFPA will focus its work in Zhemgang, one of the country's poorest districts, which has high rates of teenage pregnancies, infant and maternal deaths. Funds will be used to train health personnel to provide emergency obstetric care, develop a system to report maternal deaths, revise maternal death audit forms to ensure they include the cause of death, which will help prevent future deaths, provide clinics with reproductive health equipment, and provide young women and adolescents with reproductive health services to promote safe motherhood and help them avoid unwanted pregnancies and unsafe sex.

Half of the first million raised by the 34 Million Friends campaign is being used to address obstetric fistula, the most devastating of all pregnancy-related disabilities. Eliminated in wealthy countries, including the United States, over a century ago, fistula affects an estimated 50,000 to 100,000 women each year. It usually occurs when a young, poor woman has an obstructed labour and cannot get a Caesarean section when needed. The baby usually dies. If the mother survives, she is left with extensive tissue damage to her birth canal that renders her incontinent. Fortunately, fistula is both preventable and treatable. Delaying early pregnancy, educating young women about their bodies and providing skilled medical care at childbirth can help prevent fistula. Reconstructive surgery costs about $350 and is over 90 per cent effective if done properly. UNFPA grants to prevent and treat fistula were provided to six countries: Mali, Senegal, Nigeria, Benin, Malawi and Bangladesh. These funds were used to renovate facilities, train doctors and nurses and purchase much needed surgical equipment and supplies such as suture material, operating theatres, beds and antibiotics. Community outreach will also be undertaken to raise awareness about fistula.

Isn't that just wonderful!

A week later, on May 7, we were in Brussels to launch 34 Million Friends in the European Union (EU) at a gala performance at the Residence Palace Theater. Walter Coddington of "Face to Face" with his many ties in Europe had put the whole thing together.

My husband and I flew to Brussels on Sunday, May 4. On Monday, May 5, Lois and I taped interviews with Linda Gray, the star of the TV series "Dallas," whom Europeans adore, and who is the "Face to Face" chairwoman and UNFPA Goodwill Ambassador. We also met others of the celebrities gathered for this event which, as I understand it, was underwritten by the Packard Foundation. At lunch at a sandwich place, I met a representative of the American Friends Service Committee and another fellow from Work for Peace to whom I issued invitations for the event. — My less than shy networking skills again! That afternoon we went through a rehearsal, testing of microphones, then dinner and I practiced my short little speech until 3:00 a.m.

At breakfast on May 7, *the day*, my husband recognized Claes Nobel of the Nobel Prize family, and after Jay left to take a shower, I went and introduced myself as one of the co-founders and after a few pleasantries went back to my table. We both continued to read our newspapers, but then he invited himself for coffee at my table and I almost fainted. We had a very philosophical discussion about the meaning of life, a possible afterlife, and for him it was clear that the causes of population, women's lives and the life of the planet are some kind of mystical calling.

The DVD of the Brussels event, which I watched just recently, was thrilling. The Sinopia Dance Company provided the dance links between the interviews and other entertainment. Goodwill Ambassadors, entertainers, and television personalities took part from Portugal, Switzerland, Germany, Norway, Sweden, Finland, Denmark, and Belgium. Dr. Steven Sinding, Director General of the International Planned Parenthood Federation, was there. Thoraya Obaid was there to introduce Lois and me. The theme was "Reach 2," that this subject is too important to leave to governments alone, and that even though European governments give healthy allocations to UNFPA, the world's peoples could supplement with small gifts to announce their own conviction on the importance of supporting the women of the world.

Serendipitously again, Micol Zarb, the media person from UNFPA had gone to a gathering that day of EU reporters who were waiting for a briefing by the World Health Organization on SAARS. So she issued invitations to the whole group to come that evening to the performance. They did.

We got wonderful press coverage and a wonderful launch of 34 Million Friends in Europe. And Sheryl Snyder Savina, one of my French students at the University of Redlands in the sixties came all the way from Paris for the event.

The next evening was just as unbelievable. I don't remember exactly how this happened, but somehow Raoul Weiler, President of the Club of Rome in Brussels, had invited me to talk about 34 Million Friends at this prestigious venue. This is a "global think tank and centre of innovation and initiative. It brings together scientists, economists, businesspeople, international high civil servants, heads of state and former heads of state who are convinced that the future of humankind is not determined once and for all and that each human being can contribute to the improvement of our societies." Well, to be invited to speak to the Brussels branch of the Club of Rome was quite something. —I won't mention that it was an audience of only three. I said that the world must rededicate itself to the Programme of Action of the Cairo ICPD. I outlined what UNFPA does and shared the concept of 34 Million Friends, summarized material on Bush's war on women, the Gag Rule, defunding UNFPA, promoting "Abstinence Only" both here and abroad. Abstinence is wonderful. It removes all risks. It's only the *only* part that I object to. After all, human beings do have a very strong drive to reproduce.

I talked about the importance of access to family planning to reduce population growth – which we need if the Earth is to have a chance of sustaining itself and if there is not going to be increased human misery. Afterwards my husband and I, Raoul, and Marc Luyckx Ghisi went out for a fabulous dinner of shrimp salad, lamb chops, crème brûlée and talked about God, spirituality, women and patriarchy. Raoul and Marc wanted me to meet two people here in the USA, Riane Eisler, author of **The Chalice and the Blade** a world wide best seller that traces the history of human spirituality.

Certainly, there are historical records and artifacts that show worship of the female, the fertility goddess, the Earth Mother, etc. The more patriarchal religions have developed in fairly recent human history. Raoul and Mark also wanted me to touch base with a group called FAVORS and its founder Sergio Lub. I am in frequent touch with Riane, spent a day with her in Carmel, California and I talked to FAVORS at Sergio's home in November 2003 in Walnut Creek, California. Through the contact with Sergio and Gaye Lub, I was able to speak at the Gather the Women conference in October 2004 in Dallas, Texas.

Jay and I spent two additional days in Brussels, the highlight of which was a visit to a retrospective on the Belgian singer Jacques Brel. I know his songs by heart. I also searched out an Internet café and saw that our event had gotten very good press in Europe. Raoul Weiler and I have stayed in touch. He is very interested in spreading technology and the Internet to the third world and he put me in touch with Dr. Franz Radermacher at the University of Ulm in Germany who has conceived of a Global Marshall Plan for the world. This Global Marshall Plan movement is also sponsored by the Club of Rome. I was asked to write a commentary for the Global Marshall Plan book. My concluding paragraph reads:

"In conclusion I would say that we should first live up to the very letter of the Cairo agreement. Nothing could equal in importance the education, health, and equality of the world's women. They are the key, I think, to sustainable development, to population stabilization, to environmental and human health. They are the key also to worldwide peace and stability. Embracing women in all aspects of life has really never been tried in any concentrated fashion. The Global Marshall Plan if it embraces the women of the world will be a marvelous contribution to the world and to civilized dialog about the future of people, the planet, and the generations to come. I know Professor Radermacher feels as deeply as I do about this and will be a wonderful voice for change."

(In June 2005, Jay and I had lunch in Ulm with Professor Radermacher and several European supporters of the Global Marshall Plan.)

People from more than 30 countries have sent contributions to 34 Million Friends. In the future I hope to greatly expand this international outreach. Everyone on the planet has a stake in this. So if this book talks a little too much about 34 Million Friends, please remember that I want us all to share the vision of total equality in all human activity for all people, women and men. George Bush will pass from the scene, as will I of course, but I hope that the concept of a grassroots movement for the women and girls of the world will grow and thrive.

Above: 34 Million Friends and UNFPA press conference, Mali.
Below: Urology Department at Point G Hospital, Bamako, Mali, where Dr. Kalilou Outtara does fistula operations.

Chapter 9
Ellen, David, and Larissa

Tim Wirth, President of the UN Foundation, which was started by CNN founder Ted Turner, had announced at the press briefing that the Foundation was giving UNFPA a 25 cent match on each of the next million dollars received. Tim Wirth represented Colorado in the Congress for 18 years, the last six in the US Senate where two of his top aides were Ellen Marshall and David Harwood. Ellen and David married in the early 1990s, when they were working with Wirth at the State Department under Clinton.

Many readers will recall that Ted Turner pledged $1 billion to UN causes in 1997. The United Nations Foundation and its sister organization, Better World, were established to administer this fund.

Ellen Marshall and David Harwood, both smart thinkers and articulate writers, established the Good Works Group in Boulder, Colorado to help non-profits or grassroots efforts. The Better World Fund contracted with them to help 34 Million Friends from May 2003, until March 2005.

The Good Works Group slaved for 34 Million Friends. They had to coordinate a variety of activities with many partners. In the course of their work, they oversaw a variety of mailings to past and prospective donors. They established the wonderful www.34millionfriends.org web site. They worked with the media and engaged experts such as Cause Communications to help place articles and op-eds.

They drew up all the materials, activist kits, enrollment cards, etc. And Larissa Anstey, one of their employees, was fantastic at arranging my trips to colleges and universities. To add punch to the visits, she contacted civic groups in all the cities I was going. The *Jane's Travel Plans* documents which she would attach to emails were overflowing with every single detail I would need. Her first child was born just after 34 Million Friends became a project of Americans for UNFPA in March 2005.

David Harwood is a smart thinker and articulate writer, but I would kid him about the worst case scenarios he would depict. He was always warning me against going too far or saying something that would get us all in trouble. Lots of wisdom there.

I was in more day-to-day contact with Ellen. And Ellen was the one who somehow coordinated all materials that we had available for the million person March for Women's Lives in Washington D.C. in April 2004. She had stuff printed both in Washington and Boulder, brought enough people with her to hand out flyers, bumper stickers, and buttons to thousands. I don't know how she did it. I'll always feel close to David, Ellen, and Larissa. I still pass ideas their way to get their reaction.

Lois and I can't possibly thank the UN Foundation enough. Without its support, 34 Million Friends might have just faded away. The Foundation's support was critical in raising the next $1.7 million and kept us going until the US Committee for UNFPA became Americans for UNFPA and took us under their wing. The UN Foundation still pays for Lois' and my travel.

Chapter 10
The Computer and I

When our children, Jeffrey and Annie, were in high school, we decided that they should have access to the Internet so we signed up for AOL. Jay, my husband, had co-authored several editions of a General Chemistry lab manual but hadn't been on line so to speak. When Annie went away to Carleton College in Northfield, Minnesota (1994-1998) I learned how to do email and would email her every day some little chatty tidbit. I know that millions of parents worldwide identify with this. This continued when she went to graduate school at Berkeley. Until 2002, email was the extent of my computer skills.

So, as I said, I started by emailing the whole list of population activists but didn't know how to blind copy people so that when I sent an email to lots of people, everyone could see everyone else's email address. Blind copying is a nifty device. You just enclose all the addresses in parentheses and then put a comma between each one. Some people had a cow when I didn't do this, so I learned fast. I now have an 80 page list of email addresses of people, many of whom are real email friends. The campaign itself has gathered thousands of email addresses of people who have given permission to the campaign to send timely updates.

About a month after I sent my dollar bill, I was emailing back and forth to the US Committee for UNFPA and to Abubakar Dungus at UNFPA and I thought that I should save a few of these emails. Jay showed me how to create folders. The folders are kind of a record of the early days. I haven't saved things there in quite a while but, certainly for the first year, I saved almost all emails in folders.

Of course, I also had to start saving documents on my computer and then attaching them to email. Not hard. I also had to learn how to download documents sent to me and save those. And then throughout this effort, which has been going for three years, I have been finding web sites by Internet searches and then going to them. I love it when I see the words "Contact Us." I usually accept their kind invitation. When Al Gore was speaking years ago about an information superhighway, I had no idea what he was talking about. Now I do.

Very early in this effort, I signed up for PLANETWIRE CLIPS, a clipping service about women's health and reproductive rights and AIDS and anything at all related to population. The Communications Consortium Media Center (CCMC) in Washington D.C. headed by the incredible Kathy Bonk puts out these clips, 4 or 5 of them every day from all around the world. At the bottom of these clips one can find the address for letters to the editor. I read all of these clips religiously, and they keep me incredibly well informed. I use them to write countless letters to editors because whenever UNFPA is mentioned, or reference is made to Bush's war on women, or there is some reference to $34 million, I try to write a short pithy letter saying that to some extent 34 Million Friends has stepped into the breach and is saving lives, lessening misery and sending a nice message to the world from the American people. I may have written up to 200 letters to editors and perhaps 30 have been published. Newspapers, I think, are reluctant to print letters from outside their specific area. It's better when the letter comes from someone in the area. Recently a person unknown to me, from Oregon, had a wonderful letter in the

Oregonian informing people about 34 MF. I learned that on a weekly UNFPA summary sent out by CCMC.

List-Servs are nice. I am on a population interest list-serv with the National Audubon Society. Lively exchanges! Anyone on the list can send to the whole list with one click. Many scientists and erudite people send out their views on the environment and how population affects habitat. Many on this list-serv are very enthusiastic about 34 MF, but some have lambasted it when they learned that not every penny was going to family planning per se. Others have attacked these views with emails suggesting that reproductive health is more than just giving birth control to people. In short, very lively debates! Several groups have sent out emails about 34 MF to their list-servs. This has been a great way to spread the word.

Lois was much more aware of the power of the Internet than I was when she started her effort. She saw the exponential possibilities of email right off the bat.

At the beginning, Jay and I had just one computer between us with a dial-up system for getting on-line. To avoid divorce, we now have two computers and DSL.

What I'm going to admit now is highly embarrassing: It has just been in the last few weeks that I have learned the trick of *windows* and not closed one program to get into another one. It was while watching my daughter pulling stuff up and down when she was home from Berkeley that I realized how easy it was. It is so nice to have a trouble shooter in the house. Jay has rescued me countless times. I don't know how to use software Jay uses to make maps for me when I have to rent a car at airports and drive to nearby cities. I look at those 1000 page books for dummies and I'm smart enough to let Jay do it!

Think of all the population groups (about 10 of these), human rights groups here and abroad, women's groups, health groups, law groups, religious and church groups and religious leaders, environmental groups, groups numbering in the hundreds, and you will have some idea of the searches and outreach I have tried to do using the computer.

Our web site for October and November 2004 had 12,000 hits each month. I think that's pretty darn good.

One can get too attached to the Internet. At certain times, I have checked for email way too often and just browsed around for no good reason. And I'm kind of addicted to *exciting stuff*. With something like this grassroots effort, you want great stuff to happen so you check and check to see if maybe. I've got to watch that!

And there is such a thing as Internet etiquette. You don't forward things to unknown people whose email addresses you happen to get from others. I have sinned a few times. I've been torn between trying to get the word out and the rules of the highway.

Chapter 11
Letters from Donors and Thank You Notes

One of the greatest joys of this campaign has been reading the letters people have sent in with their contributions. Here are excerpts from five:

"When my daughter gets older I want her to have all the freedoms that women have now plus more. So here's my 2 dollars. I hope this helps. Thank you for helping change the world."

~~~

"Thank you for making a fabulous initiative to right a horrific wrong in the funding allotments of our country. Here's my birthday money from my grandma. I can't think of a better way to spend it."

~~~

"Because I can't imagine life without my mom."

~~~

"I am a Republican but this is one issue that I disagree with the President on. I have written a letter to the White House urging them to change their stand."

~~~

"This small contribution comes with prayers for the women who will benefit and even more prayers for those that suffer from lack of funds. Bless you for acting on your mission."

~~~

You can understand how responsible Lois and I feel to make sure that this money is well spent.

Another great joy has been to write and send thank you notes to the wonderful Americans out there who have participated in 34 MF and every Friday, Jennifer at the Good Works Group would summarize for me the notes that people were including with their contributions. Here are some of Jennifer's notes to me:

Knew about the problem but didn't know she could do something until now.

16 year old junior in high school. Found the website while doing a research project and was outraged. She hopes her $5 helps.

The ABC story made me sad. Thank you again from Kansas!

She graduated from the University of Redlands in 1969 and had you for a couple of French classes.

She collected money from her yoga class.

Women's ministries held a luncheon and collected an offering.

To help ease the suffering inflicted by the Bush Administration on poor women.

Zonta Club in Illinois. $123, one dollar from each member.

Heard your interview on NPR. Great job! (NPR in Chicago).

Terrorism is best fought on a personal level by offering aid and support to a world in need.

She was a Peace Corps volunteer and saw how many women have such a lack of access to adequate information and services to plan their families. This is desperately needed.

$29, a dollar from each member of her family.

A collection from members of the Unitarian Universalist Church of Las Cruces.

$1 and sent a copy of a chain letter asking for 34 MF contributions and your poem.

$1 Read about you in Glamour Magazine. Every woman has a right to choose and the right to health care!!!

A college campus sorority took up a collection and is letting other sororities know about it.

From some women friends who live around Lake Superior. They call themselves Superior Women.

$10 Not all Americans want the world to suffer while we live in

A tax preparer is asking people to donate part of their pay to him to the campaign.

$20 She hopes the March for Women's Lives will increase aware-

From a college student who is sending more than she can afford to.

A heartfelt contribution to the health care of Our Sisters around the World.

Here's to healthy mothers around the world.

Each year a small group of friends here in Minnesota celebrates the holiday season by pooling the funds we would have spent on gifts for each other and making a donation to a worthy effort we all support. This year, we have selected the 34 Million Friends campaign.

She heard you on NPR. A retired schoolteacher and her 88 year old mother will cover a donation for Laura Bush and 2 daughters and Lyn Cheney and 2 daughters. (Again, NPR in Chicago).

I wrote all of these people my personal letter. *Notice, dear readers, that many of these people do send just the one dollar we ask, or a whole group sends $1 each.* That is just what we want but we want 34 million people to do it. So I say if you have been born and survived, send at least one dollar. Or if your mother survived childbirth, or if you've had any sex education, or used any type of contraceptive, or taken a prenatal vitamin, or had a prenatal checkup, or had a mammogram or a sonogram or a pap smear, or a doctor in the delivery room, or had a test for a sexually transmitted disease, or been treated for one, or had a vasectomy (in alphabetical order!) or love your children, then think about sending a dollar to the women of the world and inviting others to do the same.

Chapter 12
The Media

Word of mouth of course is what is supposed to make a grass-roots movement work. And it has. It has probably been the most important factor. —BUT! You really need media attention too, because then huge numbers of people hear about it and they also get word-of–mouth going. ... And your effort grows exponentially.

As I mentioned before, the *Capital Times* in Madison Wisconsin wrote the first editorial in favor of 34 Million Friends. The title of the editorial was "US Women to the Rescue." Molly Ivins' column came in October 2002, and Ellen Goodman's in December 2002. Very early also in this effort, a woman named "New Hampshire Arnie" called me and did a radio interview. And Helen Palmer of WGBH in Boston called and our little interview was on "Marketplace Morning Report." There were, though, some early fizzles.

When I got to Washington for that SWOP press conference, I went first to the CCMC headed by Kathy Bonk. I knew her slightly because she had made a presentation at the Population Activist Weekend about how to get press coverage for population issues.

When I arrived, they had just hung up the phone with a representative of Bill Moyers' "NOW" show who wanted to film us the next day. Which they did. And nothing came of it; another interesting aspect of this thing: how close you can come to major publicity and then have it fizzle.

Three more fizzles: In October 2002, we evidently came very close to getting on the "TODAY" show. But we didn't. And when I got back home after the SWOP thing, I went to play my little Pub Links golf early one morning. I was driving to the golf course and listening to Susan Stamberg on NPR's "Morning Edition." She was reviewing *Embers* by Sandor Marai, which I later bought and read. —Great book!

I remember tapping the steering wheel and saying out loud, "Come on Susan, call me up!" Well, when I got back home that afternoon, my husband had left me a big note saying that a representative of Susan Stamberg had called. I think I literally started jumping up and down. (I'm, or was, 62 years old for heaven's sake, how unseemly!)

The upshot was this: I was scheduled to go up to Seattle for a 34 Million Friends event and so it was arranged that I would go to the radio station at the University of Washington at 8:00 a.m. one morning and we would have our interview. I did not close my eyes the whole night before, not for a minute. And there was a little bit of trouble getting in the place at that hour, and then for some reason the radio engineer was a little late, and it took an extra 15 minutes to get a good hook-up with New York and I could hear that Susan was kind of in a hurry and I made the mistake of rustling my notes and papers where I had put my *sound bites*.

Well, we had our interview and I was not brilliant by any means, and somehow it just didn't seem like those wonderful NPR interviews you hear on the radio. But she assured me it would be edited and on in the next day or two. I kept going to the NPR web site and doing the search for 34 Million Friends or Jane Roberts or this or that and coming up empty. She apologized. She actually thought it had been on, but our little campaign missed a big one. A week or two later, some people in New York said they heard a report about 34 Million Friends on NPR but this turned out to be from a Sierra Club member in Florida who talked about it on her affiliate. That was at least a small consolation.

The second fizzle was *Ladies Home Journal*. Lois and I had been interviewed for the story and the photographer they hired had taken his pictures. The month before our article was scheduled to appear, George and Laura were featured on the front. Sadly, our story never appeared.

And two producers for "Sixty Minutes 2" wanted to do our story but CBS turned them down.

At the time of the One Million Dollar Press Conference in New York City on May 1, 2003 we got excellent coverage with news articles in the *New York Times*, the *Los Angeles Times*, the *Chicago Tribune*, and several other newspapers. News articles though are not as effective as editorials for getting people to act. That's just a fact of life.

Oprah Winfrey's *O Magazine* did a very nice story on us in the November, 2003 issue in a section called "Circle Power." About 7 groups or pairs of women were featured who were doing good things. In several articles about Oprah, I have read that she says "Africa will be my legacy." Many people have written to Oprah asking her to invite us. Only time will tell.

I was watching Bill Moyers interview Sandra Postel of the Global Water Policy Project. I looked that up on the web and emailed her about 34 Million Friends and got a very nice reply. Several months later, I was asked to participate in the interactive section of *Grist* environmental Internet magazine. Grist asks you questions, you respond, and then later *Grist* readers post questions to which you also respond. To find out what this was all about before taking part, I went to www.grist.com and clicked on Interactive. Sandra Postel was the interactive person that week so I got in touch with her, again saying that I was to be next at *Grist*, congratulated her and asked for a formal endorsement by her of our effort. She nicely complied. And if you are at all interested in the subject of water for the planet, I urge you to visit www.globalwaterpolicy.org.

So I used something I saw on TV to make a contact, and then I knew who Sandra Postel was when the *Grist* opportunity came up. This kind of thing has happened a lot. I want to add that Cause Communications headquartered in Denver was the firm that got me the *Grist* interview. They also arranged for a nice interview and article in *In These Times*.

Before starting 34 MF I was very naïve about all the media outlets available to get news out. I suppose I thought that if something wasn't on one of the three networks, or in the *New York Times* or *Los Angeles Times* or *Chicago Tribune* that you might as well give up. Wrong! There are media outlets that reach small, very targeted markets. For instance, alumni magazines. I got my M.A. in French from Middlebury Graduate School of French in France and in the spring of 2003, I wrote the *Road Taken* back page essay, which goes to all Middlebury alumni. In 1990 I had gotten a teaching credential from the University of Redlands, and so was able to write a short essay for their famous alumni magazine, the *Och Tamale*. During my first visit to Yale University, I met David Steinberg who was starting an undergraduate publication called *P.H.: The Yale Journal of Public Health*. Result? A nice article in Volume 1, Number 1, Winter 2004. I wrote about my trip to Mali and Senegal for *CONSCIENCE Magazine*, the voice of Catholics for Free Choice which is headed by the very thoughtful Frances Kissling.

I read Susan Jacoby's book, **Free Thinkers** and got in touch with the Center for Secular Humanism whose magazine *Free Inquiry* had a special issue on population (August/September, 2004). They printed my paragraph entitled "34 Million Friends Supports Women's Health Initiatives." The November 2004 issue of *Peace Work* published by the American Friends Service Committee in

Cambridge, Massachusetts had a nice insert. The magazines and newsletters of the population groups, Population Coalition, Population Institute, Population Connection have to varying degrees publicized 34 MF.

The National Wildlife Federation is the only national environmental group which has published an article in their national magazine. —Sierra Club and National Audubon Society, what are you waiting for?

MS Magazine published a nice article about 34 MF and then chose Lois and me to be among their Women of the Year for 2003. Lois and I were thrilled with a feature article in the *Chronicle of Philanthropy*.

Mother Jones magazine sent Laura Fraser to my house for an in-depth interview. (Laura's **An Italian Affair** is a good book.) She wrote the article. It never came out in **Mother Jones**. Crazy!

Women's eNews is extra special. Founded by Rita Henley Jensen about 5 years ago, it covers all news related to women and writes informative articles often about subjects that don't otherwise get coverage. They also publish in Arabic to the Arab world. *Women's eNews* (Barbara Crossette was the writer) carried a very thorough article about our efforts and chose Lois and me as among the 21 Leaders of the 21st century for 2004. The ABC News story about which I'll speak in a minute had a clip of us at the awards ceremony at the Tribeca Rooftop in New York City.

Radio and TV have also played a role. After that first NPR Stamberg fiasco, I did have some media training. It lasted for 8 hours and they put me through every type of interview you are likely to encounter on radio, TV etc. You really must have your talking points and your sound bites, and no matter what they ask you, you say what you want to say. I learned how to sit, what to wear, basically how to *sound*.

Don't get me wrong. I am not being cynical about this at all. It's just reality. And I am always sincere, and I always tell the truth. The one thing you absolutely don't want is to get caught in an exaggeration or a lie. Heaven forbid. So I am very *very* careful to stick to what I know, which is quite a bit by now, and I try to say it well.

My first TV experience was on the "Week in Review" done by Adelphia Cable hosted by Bill Rosendahl in Los Angeles. I kept my hands still, stayed positive while trying to inspire. After the segment was over, Bill told me I had come over like pure sugar. I had to laugh at that one.

I've probably had 20 radio interviews ranging from just a minute or two to full half hours. My absolute best one was with Jerome McDonnell's "Worldview" show on WBEZ public radio in Chicago. Afterwards I listened to it on our own website and thought to myself "That is really good." At the American Public Health Association meeting in Washington (November 2004), I was going from table to table of university public health programs and met a guy from the Chicago area who at first said he hadn't heard of 34 Million Friends. At which point I told him about my visit to Northwestern, and then mentioned the Jerome McDonnell interview. "I heard you," he said with a big smile of recognition.

Not too far into this campaign, two people who had written for *PEOPLE Magazine* wanted to do a story on us. I guess the editors didn't think we were the right PEOPLE. I would have loved to be in People Magazine.

In March 2004 there was a well balanced article about international population issues in the *Christian Science Monitor* and the author, Howard La Franchi, had mentioned Bush's defunding of UNFPA. I wrote a letter to the editor and called the paper and emailed La Franchi about how to some extent 34 Million Friends had stepped into the breach. Mike Farrell wrote back that the letter would be published. Then he wrote back that it seemed to be fundraising so they had decided to pull it in favor of another letter. I wrote back that it was informational and that the American people had a right to know that this was going on. —Friendly exchanges all around. Fascinating really.

I invited them to send anonymous dollars and to tell their friends. If I just say that 34 Million Friends has to some extent stepped into the breach, then that is not the same thing as saying *Send Your Dollar*. I've had letters accepted, then rejected several times but many have been published too.

And then, very recently, there was a crazy exchange with the *New York Times*. They printed an editorial on Nov. 23, 2004 entitled "Rolling Back Women's Rights". In short it accused the administration of wanting to curtail women's access to full information and access to legal reproductive health care here in the United States if hospitals, doctors, pharmacists didn't want to furnish these services as a matter of conscience. I then wrote this letter to the Times:

"Let us never forget that the people who want to make abortion illegal again are the same who also want to limit access to contraception and information about contraception both here and abroad. Examples would be: abstinence-only funding both here and abroad, defunding the United Nations Population Fund which offers family planning, not abortion in over 140 countries, and what are now gag rules both domestic and overseas. This is basically a religious assault on women, the end result of which is more abortions, more misery, more death."

I got a call from the *Times* that the letter would be published. When the caller and I were all through making slight changes, I mentioned that I was cofounder of 34 Million Friends. She thought this was great and mentioned it to the letter page editors. My letter was then nixed because it was going to be self-serving. Self-serving, my foot! It doesn't serve me in any way. 34 MF doesn't even come up. I was mad as "all get out" to coin a phrase. Plus, I should have kept my big mouth shut! —One thing nice about writing a book is that you can publish all your unpublished LTEs!

Well, on to ABC News. Lois and I, as I've mentioned before, were ONE of the 21 Leaders for the 21st century (there were 20 others) for *Women's eNews* with an awards dinner and celebration at the Tribeca Rooftop in New York City on May 20th 2004. We learned that ABC News was going to film a story about 34 Million Friends and were meeting us in New York. What is it like to be part of a major network news report? This is what I wrote in my diary:

Thursday, May 20 was the big day. David Harwood, our Good Works Group person, flew in from Colorado and we met him and Micol Zarb, media person at the UNFPA, at our Helmsley Middletowne Hotel on E. 48th. Micol Zarb brought a birth kit which I hoped to show and explain on the ABC News interview later in the day. The hotel was very accommodating when ABC News showed up. They found a big enough room so that the *studio* could be set up.

ABC News was with us from about 11:00 a.m. until 9:00 p.m., in other words through the *Women's eNews* awards dinner. They did about a one hour interview with Lois and me, then filmed us on the streets of New York and at Central Park. Micol furnished them tapes of my visits to Senegal and Mali and Lois' to East Timor and Nicaragua and tape of Alvaro's visit to our homes. I even sent Nils Kongshaug, the producer, a picture of me writing thank-you notes to donors in my living room. (He had asked for it). On our way to the dinner at the Tribeca Rooftop in New York I must admit I had to laugh when my cell phone rang and it was ABC News telling us they were going to film our arrival, but we were to pay no attention and pretend they weren't there. Of course, when we did arrive and got out of the car, someone blocked their view so we had to do it *spontaneously* again. The event is *Women's eNews'* big fund raiser for the year and as I understand it, dinner was $500 but each of us 21 women could invite a guest so Annie came down from Connecticut. The Tribeca Rooftop is an elegant venue. (I hate that word, whatever happened to "place"!) The UN

Foundation and Americans for UNFPA were there in force. Dungus in his magnificent blue robe and three or four others of our special UNFPA friends also attended.

The hors d'oeuvre were magnificent and I introduced Nils to Phyllis Oakley who is Board Chairperson for Americans for UNFPA. She has worked for the State Department for both Republican and Democratic administrations and was President Clinton's State Department spokesperson. At the dinner I sat next to Eve Ensler, whose name I kind of recognized but when I realized she was the author of the *Vagina Monologues*, I was able to tell her that the University of Redlands had put on a benefit performance for 34 Million Friends.

The one meeting which meant the most to me was that of Byllye Avery (another of the 21 women) who has her own Institute for Social Change and who has headed and worked all her life for the Black Women's Health Imperative. She and I really hit it off. I certainly felt very warmly towards her and she handed me a $20 bill for 34 MF and said she would get a link on their web site. (I sent her $20 for her Institute also!) Since that evening we have been in touch. I also talked to Shahnaz Bokhari from Pakistan. She has donated a safe house for women who suffer abuse, including having acid thrown in their face if they *dishonor* the family by even looking at a man. She seemed interested in our idea of getting small donations from many many *many* people. I recently read of a woman in Pakistan whose husband cut off her feet because she ran away from his abuse.

It was pins and needles waiting for that ABC segment to be on. This is what I wrote: "I thought the segment on 34 Million Friends was going to be on this Sunday." That is what Nils Konghaug at ABC thought too. Much of the week I spent emailing my list and calling several friends to say ABC News was going to air the piece. But very late, I got word that the segment had been put off for another week because of the situation in the Darfur region of the Sudan. If you want to see how tough women have it in poor countries with conflicts over resources and power and religion, then this is a perfect example. Women being raped, forced to flee with their babies and children into refugee camps. UNFPA works in refugee camps all around the world to ease somewhat the terror and suffering. So that is OK, ABC News. You do what you have to do. I watched their 3 minute section on the Sudan tonight (June 21, 2004) and I must say it probably is more important than our little story, but our little story deals with the exact same issues concerning the plight of the women of the world.

I think I will promise myself never to forewarn people unless I get a confirmation at the start of the program or something. One must be *so* patient. You see there is no definite time limit on our story.

Above: This 16-year old girl is anticipating a third surgery to repair her vesico-vaginal and recto-vaginal fistulas at the Lamorde Teaching Hospital in Niamey, Niger. Because of extensive nerve damage, she arrived at the hospital needing a stick to help her walk. *Photo by Lisa Russell.*

July 16, 2004. They announced. *No funding* for UNFPA this year. What a tragedy. I was going to have a press conference on the phone with news writers yesterday, but of course it was cancelled. I think Lois will have her conference with editorial writers today. We knew this was coming but it is mind-bogglingly awful, causing such needless suffering. Colin Powell really has sold his soul. I've spent the last two days alerting people that this announcement was coming. I'm kind of numb, but am going to Los Angeles for "A Mother's Promise" function this afternoon. The Izaak Walton League, with an Internet petition signing campaign, has tried to get millions of Americans to support the Cairo Consensus.

July 17. Well finally! ABC News came through with a wonderful piece which lasted darn close to 5 minutes and images of the woman in labor lying on a donkey cart made it to national television. When I came up to check email about 5:00 p.m., a bunch of *our people* had seen it on the east coast. I was so afraid this would be a fizzle too. But with the determination made to deny funding again, ABC News had its "news hook" as they call it.

ABC News-WORLD NEWS TONIGHT SATURDAY
(06:30 PM ET); July 17, 2004 Saturday

HEADLINE: Medical Aid Denied US Withholds Funds for Poor Women BOB WOODRUFF, ABC NEWS

(Off Camera) We learned this week that for the third year in a row the Bush Administration will withhold millions of dollars from a United Nations program that helps poor women around the world get reproductive health care. More than 40 percent of women in developing countries deliver their babies without medical help and many thousands of them die because of it. So, when the US first cut funding for this program, many people complained and two American women began doing something about it.

BOB WOODRUFF (Voice Over) When New Mexico attorney Lois Abraham heard the news, she was angry. In California, retired French teacher Jane Roberts was angry, too. What made them angry was the decision by the Bush Administration to pull the funding for the United Nations Population Fund, the UNFPA, which provides health care and family planning to poor women around the world.

JANE ROBERTS, FORMER TEACHER (showing safe birth kit) UNFPA distributes these in remote villages where there are no trained midwives, no trained doctors. It consists of a sterile plastic sheet, a bar of soap, a razor blade to cut the umbilical cord and string to tie it off. And it saves thousands and thousand of lives every year. Basic health care, just basic stuff.

LOIS ABRAHAM, ATTORNEY These are activities which fill needs, real needs that most Americans can't even understand because we are so fortunate.

BOB WOODRUFF (Voice Over) When the US pulled its funding in 2002, the UNFPA lost $34 million a year, a substantial chunk of its budget.

JANE ROBERTS I said, shoot, I'll try to get 34 million people to give one dollar.

LOIS ABRAHAM We complemented each other.

JANE ROBERTS We complemented each other, absolutely.
BOB WOODRUFF (Voice Over) They named their effort "34 Million Friends" and just two years later ...

LOIS ABRAHAM We are very close to $2 million.

BOB WOODRUFF (Voice Over) Abraham and Roberts were honored recently in New York for their fund-raising success. (Shot of

awards at Women's eNews event) Though they admit it's just a frac-
tion of what the UNFPA has lost. So why did the US pull funding
for a UN program to help poor women in the first place? The
answer is wrapped up in the issue and the politics of abortion.

JANE ROBERTS UNFPA does not do abortions. They don't believe
in abortion as a method of family planning.

BOB WOODRUFF (Voice Over) But critics charge the organization
was supporting programs in China, where the goal is one child per
woman, that coerced women into having abortions. Newspaper
editorials around the country condemned the US decision to pull
its funding, calling it more about abortion politics than policy.
The State Department sent a fact-finding team to China. It found
no evidence that the UNFPA participated in a program of coercive
abortion. But the money has still not been restored. Both women
have traveled to the places where their money is being spent.
Nicaragua, East Timor, Africa.

JANE ROBERTS We came across a woman on a donkey cart who
was in labor. And a little boy was driving the donkey and she knew
there was the clinic, she knew that that's where she should go to
give birth safely. The doctor who was with us, he turned his truck
around and drove her to the clinic. I gave birth at age 35, and I
was so grateful for care before during and after. And I know that
the women of the world, many of them have none of this.

LOIS ABRAHAM It's worlds apart, and it shouldn't be worlds apart.
We want to move those worlds a little closer together.

BOB WOODRUFF (Off Camera) We should say the Administration
says it would consider money for the UN population fund if China
changes its government family planning policies. We'll be right
back. commercial break

<< ABC News World News Tonight — 7/17/04 >>

34 Million Friends~101

I believe 34 Million Friends has not had the media attention it deserves. One reason might be that it is extremely political.
It goes directly against the Administration. But it is not Lois and
Jane who are political, it is the Administration that adopts spuri-
ous positions that fly in the face of world opinion, common
sense, and decency.   That's my view.

But,   there are more reasons the media have been a little
reluctant to give 34MF the access it deserves.   Many in the media
consider 34 Million Friends a *women's issue*, soft news, a little too
cute.   Not true. This is serious business. The underlying issues are
the most profound facing all peoples, the planet, and the future of
both. There is no such thing as a women's issue.   These are fully
human issues in the most profound sense and need to be covered
by the media very PROFOUNDLY.

Above: (left to right) Jane, woman with child, and Younes Zouglami, a Tunisian
who is head of UNFPA mission in Mali. Below: Jane meets District Governor
and Imam at UNFPA clinic in Senegal.

Chapter 13
My Travels
a very personal journey

Doris Haddock, in her book *Granny D* described her walk across the country (I think she was in her nineties) for campaign finance reform, in an effort to encourage a grassroots movement to take hold. My wonderful friend Evelyn Ifft insisted that I read the book. I wrote down some very inspiring words such as: "When you fully dedicate yourself to a good mission, then the floodgates of heaven open up for you." And, "We are all dying, and we might as well be spending ourselves in a good cause." And, "Never be discouraged from being an activist because people tell you that you'll not succeed. You have already succeeded if you're out there representing the truth or justice, or compassion, or fairness, or love." Right on Granny D! I'm just glad I don't have to walk across the country for my cause!

I was aching to talk to people about 34 Million Friends and the UN Foundation seemed to want to give me the chance by supporting my travel. I can't possibly share with you all the rich experiences I've had, the lovely moments with people, the dedication of idealistic students who want to pitch in for the women of the world. Here are just some very human highlights, not in chrono-logical order.

I met Jan Holmgren, President of Mills College in Oakland, because she was hosting the National Council of Research on Women conference on her campus. Thoraya Obaid, Executive Director of the UNFPA, was class of 1966 at Mills and is on the Board of Trustees. Small world!

I went with Ellen Marshall of Good Works Group to the office of Sono Aibe, the Packard Foundation's point person for popula-tion. It was in that office in Los Altos, California that I thought of writing a poem which could possibly be put to music for 34MF. I wrote it on an airplane. The legendary Odetta has sung a song based on this poem. Listen to the song-DVD on our web site. Here's the poem. To me it epitomizes everything good about UNFPA.

WE are 34 million friends
We ARE 34 million friends
We are 34 MILLION friends
Of the women of the world

We are reaching out to the world
We are going to have our say
We are reaching out to the world
Through the UNFPA

Every baby welcome now
Loved and fed and vaccinated
Mothers children learning now
Reading writing educated

Every child a heartfelt joy
Every child a book and toy
Every child with wings unfurled
Whether it be boy or girl

No more death while giving birth
Because a midwife's taking care
No more mothers in the earth
Because a midwife's helping there

To AIDS and violence we say NO
To family planning we say YES
Human rights are the way to go
Surely we can do no less

Woman lying on a donkey cart
Dirt road heat wave and in labor
Doctor put her in his truck
Luck that day was in her favor

And all of us who have so much
One dollar we can share
To show the women of the world
That we the people care

We are 34 Million Friends
And we are going to have our say
We are reaching out to the world
Through the UNFPA

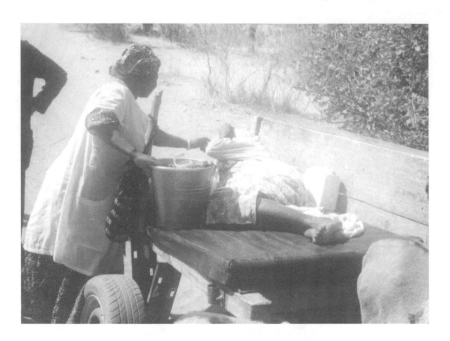

Above: Woman in labor on donkey-cart. Jane met this woman on the road as she was in labor and being taken to a clinic. Jane asked to take her picture, promising that people all over the world would see her and want to help women in need.

In June 2003, I was at the American Association of University Women conference in Providence, Rhode Island. I arrived at the bottom of an escalator just as about 200 delegates came down after a plenary session. I handed out orange cards like mad saying I was going to give a presentation on this later in the conference. Jane Stanley told me at a reception the first night that a little blurb I had sent her was going to be in the *California Perspective* that goes to 17,000 people. Wonderful.

On June 21, I got my 34 MF display set up in the Bristol Room of the Providence Convention Center and then attended as many sessions as possible to put in my two cents. AAUW is a stupendous organization. They work on education for girls and women particularly in science and technology and are a global voice for gender equity.

One afternoon I took a taxi to the Roger Williams Memorial, then walked up Benefit Street seeing the old 17th century houses along the way. I then went into the First Baptist Church where one of the architects was a James Sumner. Sumner is the middle name of my father, Joseph Sumner Keeney, born in Rockville, Connecticut in 1898. And then on the Brown campus I found the Keeney Triangle. No relation, but good New England names. On the huge lawn of the Brown campus, sitting on a bench was a young man reading the *Odyssey*. I sat down and we started chatting. Corey Byrnes had just graduated in East Asian Studies, had spent one year and three summers in China and was headed for Cambridge in England on a Rhodes type scholarship. We remain in touch and when I gave him an orange card I was delighted that he assured me he had given to 34 Million Friends. —My niece Janea is at Brown now, does pole vaulting on the track team!

On August 17, 2003, I flew to Santa Fe, New Mexico for picture taking for Oprah's magazine with Lois who was coming down from Taos. That evening I chose the Café de Paris for dinner because when walking by a garage, I saw two people coming out carrying instruments. They turned out to be French musicians, the entertainment for the restaurant. Naturally I told them why I was in Santa Fe. Among their friends at a table was a Santa Fe ob-gyn physician who had heard about 34 Million Friends and who had sent a contribution. She radiated enthusiasm. —I also got to sing along to the Jacques Brel and Juliette Greco songs.

In the morning Roy and John, the photographers, drove Lois and me out to White Rock overlooking the Rio Grande. What that scene has to do with 34 MF I have no idea, but out of the 50 pictures the fellows snapped, there was at least one good one which is on p. 267 of the November 2003 *O Magazine*.

In late October 2003, I started on a real adventure. I was both excited and nervous about this undertaking. It was more than a one stop trip! First, I flew to Ottawa, Canada for the Tenth Canadian Conference on International Health where I addressed a large student affiliate group and networked with the conference, particularly making a wonderful contact with Médecins Sans Frontières. While there, I heard reports on ABS (Acid Burn Survivors), women who are *punished,* often by their own family members, for some perceived *faux pas* which *dishonors* the family. I saw slides. UGH! I also learned that women in Costa Rica grow, spray, and ship the ferns which are part of our flower bouquets in the US. There are an inordinate number of birth defects among their children due to heavy use of pesticides.

Then, a flight down to Minneapolis where David Paxson of World Population Balance was a wonderful help, driving me to appointments at both the *Pioneer Press* and the *Minneapolis Star Tribune*. The latter featured in their Sunday editorial section a big Question-and-Answer with me, accompanied by a lovely large picture. This produced a sea of contributions from ordinary people and a wonderful contribution from the Minneapolis Chapter of AAUW.

I spoke at three colleges in the Minneapolis area, at Carleton College in Northfield, where my daughter graduated in 1998, to a number of students in the medical school at the University of Minnesota arranged by a friend of my daughter, and at a Catholic college, St. Benedict's, where some very courageous girls fought with the college administration to have me come. Free speech was their argument which evidently won the day, although my talk was attended by only students. I met no administrator or faculty member while there. The girls did invite me, though, for a dorm-cooked spaghetti dinner to die for.

Thanks to the stubbornness of David Paxson and the outreach of Cause Communications, I had an interview with Don Shelby on October 28, on WCCO radio, a highly rated drive-home-from-work station. And, quite funny really, because I had spent the night with the Paxsons instead of at my scheduled motel, I had missed a message that I was supposed to meet with a Stu Ackman from the United Nations Association in the morning before flying out. At the airport, sitting on the john, in midstream literally, my cell phone rang and I struggled to answer it. We have a good 10 minute conversation where I was taking a few notes and half way giggling at my situation, and wondering what all the women waiting in line were thinking.

My next visit was to the University of Virginia Law School for a late afternoon address on October 30. Jon Cannon, former general counsel to the Environmental Protection Agency introduced me and there I was at this most prestigious law school, (think Thomas Jefferson!) talking to both students and faculty in the glorious rotunda. Every day I am in awe of what has become of Lois' and my crazy idea.

Arriving in Philadelphia on Halloween, my taxi driver was in the process of telling me how Halloween was the devil's work when we arrived at the home of Buck and Mary Scott who had put out some 50 pumpkins, ghosts, and spider webs all over their front porch.

The next day Buck and Mary escorted me to the United Nations Association luncheon on the Bryn Mawr campus where I accepted for Lois and me a Global Citizenship award. I also spoke at Swarthmore where some foreign students who were active in the Rotary affiliate, Rotaract, had tabled for a week, gathered a big turn-out for my talk, and handed me a pile of student dollars after the event.

Shira Abeles invited me to speak to medical students at Columbia and her sister Adina invited me to address the Bren School of Environmental Science at the University of California at Santa Barbara. These two sisters had no idea what the other was doing. Amazing.

Yale! Yes, well, my Yale story is quite something. On the airplane flying over to Santa Fe for the *O Magazine* picture, I was sitting next to a high school student and his mother. She was reading the *New Yorker* so I figured she probably wasn't some extreme right-winger. When her son said to her, "Hey Mom, trade magazines with me," I took the opportunity to pipe up, "Speaking of magazines, I'm on my way to have my picture taken by....etc."

Well, the woman was Dr. Kristi Lockhart, professor at Yale. Her husband, Dr. Frank Keil, is the Master of one of the undergraduate colleges at Yale, Morse College. My dad graduated from Yale in 1921 and, then, taught at Yale in China in 1922. The upshot was that I was invited to address the Master's Tea at Morse College of Yale University and also to spend the night in the Master's House. This was special to me because of my Dad. I even walked over to the Yale in China office and saw my Dad's name on their data base.

Before my talk, I had lunch with two students, David Steinberg and Grace Yuen, both AIDS activists. The article I later wrote for *Public Health Magazine,* founded by David, was "Human Numbers, Human Beings." The stress was on the 1.2 billion adolescents on the planet and what this means for them and for the planet.

This same trip involved visiting Maine's Bowdoin College where Anne Morlan, the widow of my mentor at the University of Redlands, came to hear me. After Bob Morlan died, she studied for the ministry and was for several years the pastor of a small church. Her son Larry had graduated from Bowdoin. The next day I drove way up to Unity College, a college almost exclusively dedicated to environmental studies. I shared the podium with the wonderful Julie Starr of the National Wildlife Federation.

It was a two week trip and I called my husband every night using my cell phone which was totally new for me. Guess what, the last four digits are 3434.

The only bad thing that happened during this trip (bad is a very relative term, right?) was that I flew into Portland, Maine at night, rented my car and couldn't for the life of me find the motel where a room was booked. My maps seemed to bear no relation to what was on the ground. Finally, I got on the toll freeway and the toll guy told me what to do, go north, get off, go south etc. I had been in tears and swearing a blue streak. You can all relate to that, I think!

During the Iraq debate at the UN, I happened to be in New York and saw an ad in the *New York Times* from about 150 religious leaders stating that, "We, religious leaders, stand firmly in support of the United Nations and are grateful for the leadership of Secretary-General Kofi Annan during these challenging times." I obtained the contact information from as many as I could and emailed them or even wrote some snail mail letters. When I saw Reverend Dr. James Forbes (whose name appeared on the *New York Times* list) on Bill Moyers' "NOW" program, I knew I would like to meet him. I made a special trip with frequent flyer miles to New York for an event at Reverend Forbes' magnificent Riverside Church to commemorate Roe vs. Wade. Dan Maguire, author of *Sacred Choices* and head of the Religious Consultation on Population, Reproductive Health, and Ethics, was the main speaker.

After the service, I was thrilled to get a hug from Reverend Forbes. Our daughter Annie took the train from Connecticut to meet me for this evening service. Wonderful! —She's a mother's dream. We have such fun

Our cabdriver back to the hotel was a Pakistani who was on the night shift and promised to pick me up at 4:30 a.m. for my trip to the airport. He did. Thank you, out there somewhere!

On March 6, 2004, I spoke at the University of Oregon's Environmental Law Conference. Checking out of my motel, I struggled with two suitcases, my briefcase, and other *stuff,* trying to open the door going into the motel lobby. There was a man standing on the other side of the door who didn't lift a finger. Good choice on his part because after checking out and sitting down to wait for my ride to the airport, a woman in her seventies seated across the way piped up, "If that had been my son, I'd have wrung his neck." "It did seem a little strange," I said, "because if he had been in my place, I certainly would have helped him." Upshot? Her husband sitting next to her was a retired ob-gyn who had worked for Planned Parenthood. They were in Eugene because their son, also an ob-gyn who had done the abortions in his medical group, had been killed five years earlier in a traffic accident. They were there to meet the young person who was to be the recipient of the scholarship they had established in their son's name.

I told them why I was there and guess what? Yep! "Are you Jane Roberts? How wonderful! I've given to this more than once. Please give me those orange cards. I'm going to spread this far and wide." So you see how lucky I was that an oaf hadn't helped me, and I think the couple and I felt a real kinship upon parting.

Down to Portland, Oregon. Ramona Rex and Albert Kaufman are two tigers of the reproductive health and family planning community. Albert is very active with Population Connection which used to be Zero Population Growth (ZPG). Ramona is active in the Population and Development section of the Sierra Club. I had met them before in Washington D.C. and they had been long-time email buddies. They had arranged for me to talk at the very wonderful First Unitarian Church in Portland. For this trip I had forgotten to take my cell phone, so before the talk I called Colorado early in the afternoon to see if anything was cooking. Yes, I was supposed to do a half hour long radio interview with Michelle at KBOO radio which was to be rebroadcast on International Women's Day, March. 8. —Whew, glad I checked.

On March 16, 2004, I flew to Atlanta. I was to rent a car and drive straight to Macon, Georgia. The night before my flight, I happened to check to see if my driver's license was where it should be, in a rubber band with my credit cards in a zipped pocket of my purse. Not there.

How can you rent a car without driver's license? Utter panic. I sometimes put it in my briefcase in a zipped section with my airline e-tickets so I looked there, dumped everything out. Not there. Utter frustration. I knew I wouldn't sleep the whole night. I put my passport in my purse to be able to, at least, get on the plane. What in hell (pardon my French) was I going to do? Impossible. That just can't happen.

I was in the shower when my husband yelled "Found it". It had been face down next to the bed near where I had dumped the briefcase stuff. Heavens!

On the plane I met a really nice architect who designs FOBs, flight operation something-or-others. I don't know what the B stands for but anyway hangars, fuel stations for private planes. I explained about 34 Million Friends and with no prompting, he used the same two terms I use for the Bush decision: "small-minded, mean-spirited." What a coincidence! He handed me $20 and his name is on the web.

Landing in Atlanta I rented my car and drove to Macon, Georgia. To make a long story short, I spoke at wonderful Wesleyan College, a women's college where Catherine Meeks, the Executive Director of the Student Service Center was going to invite all students to give a dollar.

I got on the freeway back to Atlanta and actually didn't make any mistakes driving to the offices of GCAPP headed by Michelle Ozumba. GCAPP stands for Georgia Campaign for Adolescent Pregnancy Prevention. (Jane Fonda was one of *Women's eNews'* Women of the Year in 2004 for her work with this agency.) I walked from there to the *Atlanta Journal and Constitution* downtown to drop off a nice informational packet for Cynthia Tucker, who heads up the editorial pages and writes her own column. Maybe her paper will write again about this. With my good maps and lots of luck I drove to Emory University—in fact right to the guest parking lot, which was closest to the building where I was speaking.

Julie Marie Goupil, a public health student was my contact. She and I had regaled ourselves by trading emails in French. Her mother was there to help set up and the talk was very well attended. Serendipitously, a group of UNIFEM people were meeting upstairs so we all worked it out that I could also go up there and present 34 MF to a whole roomful of women from the community.

A bunch of girls and I then went out for pizza. I got lost driving back in the dark and ended up driving through the Carter Center (Freedom Parkway) to reach my airport motel for an early flight out. I had written President Carter earlier about 34 Million Friends and joked in my letter that with the projected 9 billion people on the planet in 50 years, Habitat for Humanity would never be able to "keep up"!

Supporting UNFPA is baseball, motherhood, apple pie and patriotism all together.

I landed in Madison, Wisconsin on April 8 and was picked up by Marisa Rinkus of the National Wildlife Federation. She is their representative in the Midwest and is a tremendous networker. Several college students attend a Washington NWF sponsored symposium every year and Sarah Craven of UNFPA briefs them on UNFPA and population issues. Several of my college visits have been organized by these idealistic NWF students. Anna Corey had done the impossible by getting a big turnout at Lawrence University in Wisconsin.

In setting up my talk, there was no table high enough for my slide projector to project onto the screen so we put a table on a table with disastrous results. Somehow, the table on top slipped off the table on bottom and naturally landed on my slide projector which had slipped off first. Crash. Tray broken and automatic button for next slide not working, so for the rest of the trip it was an awkward clumsy do-it-by-hand effort. Fortunately, the slides could still be seen even if only sort of!

The next morning Marisa drove me in NWF's Toyota Prius to Madison, Wisconsin. On the way down we stopped at a couple of camera places to check for available Leica slide projectors but to no avail. Later in the afternoon, I walked down to the Electric Earth Café to meet Erika Norris, the University of Wisconsin organizer and several other students for an informal meeting. A bunch of us all went out for kabobs for dinner. Caroline Beckett of National Audubon drove both copies of my signed credit card form back to the restaurant. The waitress probably thought that 11 people had stiffed her!

On Saturday morning, I flew to Chicago's O'Hare airport. My taxi driver to the Millennium Knickerbocker was an African American, who had done many things in his life including graphic design. He would vote for Kerry because Kerry was a Vietnam veteran and so was he. He promised to look up 34 MF on the web. I'm sure he did.

After dinner I visited Kinko's to check on email and learned that a letter from me would be printed in *E/The Environmental Magazine*. Every little bit helps! I also learned that a letter I had written to the Cornell Daily Sun would get in that university's newspaper just under the wire. Good!

I had a weekend free in Chicago, Easter weekend. I was jazzed to be able to take walks, read my book (**Granny D**) and watch the Masters Golf, which I did by the hour. On one walk, I scouted out where my talk to Northwestern medical students would be on East Superior Ave.

Whenever I'm traveling for 34 MF, I can't really think about anything else so I don't go to shows or sightsee or anything. I find that I mostly practice speeches and try to think of new ways to say old things.

People from the UN Foundation were in charge of my Chicago visit so I was taken everywhere, which made it really easy. Katy took me to my noon meeting with medical school students at Northwestern organized by John Broach, the International Health Chair. After the talk, I visited with Mame from Senegal who was in her 6th year at the medical school. It was a lunch meeting so the group had brought in burritos and soft drinks. All 35 students seemed alert and interested. Of course, they know about obstetric fistula.

Monday evening I was out on the campus of Northwestern at Evanston, again at a meeting organized by a student, Charlotte Smith. It's hard to know how much carry through comes of these meetings, but, let's face it, it takes very few students to take the message of 34 MF to an entire campus. But, they have to do it. I certainly have the distinct impression that their hearts are in it.

Tuesday, April 13 was a wild day with 4 different functions. At 7:45 a.m. I was driven to Dupage College in Aurora where I talked to 90 students from 4 different classes and got my slide projector to work pretty well. I felt I was really good and the reaction was terrific. One of the several classes was a class in Ethics, and I believe there was a Women's Studies class, and a foreign language class. I always try to stress how wonderful it was to be able to speak French in Senegal and Mali.

Then it was on to a meeting in a town belonging to House Speaker Dennis Hastert's district. There were many members from AAUW including a Cheryl Anderson who had seen my display and heard me speak a little in Providence, Rhode Island, at the AAUW conference. She is on the national board and the Illinois State Board of AAUW and she just sparkles when talking about 34 MF. There were also representatives of a business women's group and from Rotary. —Did you know that Rotary International has done more for eradicating polio in the world than anyone else? Rotary has also established the RIPD, the Rotary Initiative for Population and Development.

Then it was back to Chicago for an interview with Jerome McDonnell on WBEZ, Chicago NPR. He has a program about international affairs that runs weekdays from 1:00 to 2:00 p.m.. I thought I did OK, never as brilliant as I would like to be, especially as he had to tell me to stop tapping my pen on the table. — After my media training no less! I did recite my poem, asked him first if he wouldn't mind, told him probably this was the first time someone had recited a poem on his show.

He said the program would air within a month and our web site would be on their web site for quite a while. I did say that supporting UNFPA should be a social contract with the world and used my baseball analogy of the Bush administration being over the fence in right field. UNFPA, I say, plays centerfield, absolutely mainstream.

I will have to now tell you about an extraordinary airport meeting. Honestly, if I were to just catch planes around the country, 34 MF would not do too badly.

OK, so I'm at O'Hare flying over to East Lansing, Michigan for a meeting with students at Michigan State University (MSU). I get to the airport early, much less stress that way. I sit down at the gate for small commuter jets and next to me is Emma Hughes, from a small town in Indiana, a charming, energetic woman 3 days short of her 90th birthday. She has been in Chicago visiting her daughter. She reminds me of what *Granny D* must be like. We talked about everything and I gave her my famous orange card. Her daughter, she laments, is a Bush lover. She, on the other hand, volunteers that Bush's press conference on Iraq was a lot of rhetoric, that abortion is necessary sometimes, that it's between a woman, her doctor, her God. Government has no business. — What prompted this was my mild remark that UNFPA did no abortions. Then she said that God had given her many gifts and that she is grateful. She has friends, she says, who will look up www.34millionfriends.org for her.

"You're a lovely lady, Mrs. Hughes," I say.

"And you are another friend I've added to my life, dear Jane." We are both utterly sincere.

She gets up to tape her toe, which is sore, and soon a distinguished but slightly rumpled "seventyish" man comes up and sits down leaving an empty chair between us. "A long walk," he says. If anyone knows O'Hare you know what he means.

"Sure is," I say.

"Are you going to East Lansing?"

"Yes".

"So am I. You look rather professorial. Are you a professor at MSU?"

"No, but I am a professor at MIT (Massachusetts Institute of Technology)." (I go GULP.)

"You know," I say, "scientists aren't too happy with the Bush administration for often ignoring sound science in its environmental policies. The Union of Concerned Scientists just released a letter in this regard."

"I was one of the people who signed the letter."

I then made this statement. "You are a Nobel Laureate."

"Yes," with a slight smile, "I am."

"What did you discover?"

"Quarks!" Well, to make a long story short, Dr. Jerome Friedman, Nobel Laureate in physics and I had a good 20 minute discussion about all and everything and I got out my material, showing him the safe birth kit, the elementary school booklet, with the equality for little girls message, the Kristof editorial in the *New York Times* which said we were making valiant efforts for maternal health.

He generously allowed that we could use his name as endorsing our efforts. Then Emma came back and sat between us and I introduced the two of them. I had already told him about this marvelous encounter with Emma. He was as impressed as I had been. We three had a great time shooting the breeze. —Several months later when I spoke at the Harvard Center for Population and Development Studies, Jerome and his warm wonderful wife Tania came to hear me.

The March for Women's Lives on Sunday, April 25, 2004 at the Washington Mall drew one million people. Molly Ivins had written a column on April 21 about the March saying it was "not just about choice on abortion but literally about life or death for women all over the globe." She included a nice push for 34 Million

Friends calling me "the embodiment of all the Mrs Witherspoons of our lives." About a month before, I had read that she was going to be speaking in Pasadena, California. I had contacted Creators Syndicate to ask if I could possibly meet with her. We had dinner together before her talk.

About 50 representatives from foreign countries came to the March to say how Bush policies of taking away family planning money because of the Gag Rule and Abstinence Only policies, and defunding of UNFPA had hurt and even killed women in their countries. On September 30, 2003, *Agence France-Presse* had head-lined an article "Council of Europe Calls on Bush to Lift Ban on Overseas Family Planning Aid." This article referred to the Gag Rule and the Council's parliamentary assembly, which voted 89 to 8 to ask the Bush Administration to rescind it, said that the cut-off of aid was contributing to more unwanted pregnancies and abortions.

Unwanted pregnancies and illegal unsafe abortions in poor countries result in the deaths of poor vulnerable women.

I was so pleased that this March wasn't just for choice for American women but for women's access to quality reproductive health care all over the world. It was for CHOICE in a very expand-ed sense of the term. Late in the afternoon, all of these represen-tatives carried their flags onto the stage. I carried the American flag. I was so proud! My Annie was with me.

There were lots of activities surrounding the March. People from the UN Foundation, the CCMC, Good Works Group and many more were everywhere handing out buttons and materials. At CCMC I had the great pleasure of shaking the hand of Betty Freidan. I had spoken to her briefly on a plane from Chicago to Washington many years before. We had both been heading to the very first March for Women's Lives.

In May 2004, the Population Institute whose president is the indefatigable Werner Fornos, sponsored the Global Population Forum at Loews L'Enfant Plaza hotel in Washington D.C. World experts, really top people, shared valuable insights for 2 days. As far as I could tell, there was no publicity! Someone had even stolen all the printed materials for the conference the night before from the locked conference room. Hmmm.

At the reception for the participants at the Capitol, I spoke with Dr. Ana Lapcevic from Croatia. I asked her if she had ever visited the US before. She hadn't. She recounted the pages and pages one has to fill out to get a visa to enter the US these days. "Well," I said, "let's not stand here, let's jump in a cab, take it to the Lincoln Memorial and walk back towards the Capitol."

It was light quite late and the Mall was bathed in a soft early evening light. Ana has two children in their teens. Her husband had had a brain tumor after the second child was born, and he is extremely incapacitated. Ana and I shared our lives, our joys, and setbacks. She heads the Center for Education and Counseling for Women in Croatia. Women are amazing.

In early June, 2004 I attended a bit of the Global Health Council Conference in Washington doing on-site registration at the Omni-Shoreham Hotel. The conference theme was "Youth and Health, Generation on the Edge." I attended a morning session where Thoraya Obaid chaired a distinguished panel on the ravages of coercive early marriages on the lives of young girls. She also presented the new UNFPA film: "Too Brief a Child: Voices of Married Adolescents."

Here is UNFPA's Press Release :

Washington D.C., Leaders from UNFPA, the Population Council, the Government of Senegal and the International Center for Research on Women met today to address the neglected issue of child marriage. Child marriage violates the human rights of million of girls by threatening their health, restricting their education and limiting their social, economic and political growth.

Most nations have declared 18 as the legal minimum age for marriage. Yet, in the next decade, more than 100 million girls worldwide will marry before their 18th birthday. Some will be as young as 8 or 9 and many will marry against their will.

Married adolescents have been largely ignored in the development and health agenda because of the perception that their married status ensures them a safe passage to adulthood, said Thoraya Ahmed Obaid, Executive Director of UNFPA, the United Nations Population Fund. "Nothing could be further from the truth."

Ms. Obaid spoke at a special session of the Global Health Council's annual conference in Washington, D.C. The theme of the conference was "Youth and Health: Generation on the Edge." Other panelists included Aminata Diallo, Minister of Health, Senegal; Geeta Rao Gupta, President, International Center of Research on Women; Judith Bruce, Director, Gender, Family and

Development of the Population Council; and Kakenya Ntaiya, a young Kenyan woman who fought hard to delay marriage and continue her education.

"UNFPA seeks to reposition the concern about adolescent girls from a relatively narrow one, focused on their fertility and health, to one that emphasizes the capacities and life skills they need to negotiate their lives," said Ms. Obaid. "Income-generating work can transform the lives of married adolescents by providing them with a degree of autonomy, mobility, and freedom from traditional gender roles."

The Executive Director called for greater action to discourage child marriage, such as:

1. Highlighting the increased risk of HIV infection for young girls who marry much older men, especially in communities with high prevalence of HIV/AIDS.

2. Fostering national and community dialogue over the human dignity and human rights of all persons, and the security and health threats entailed in forced or early marriage of girls.

3. Helping girls to complete their secondary education and working to address the root causes of early marriage, such as poverty and discrimination against girls.

4. Designing safe, appropriate and effective educational skill-building, and livelihood opportunities for unmarried girls that may assist them in deferring marriage by raising their literacy, increasing their income generation and overall economic and social well-being.

Child marriage remains a deeply entrenched custom in many countries. Parents want to secure their daughters' future both socially and financially, and ties between families and villages are often strengthened with arranged marriages.

At the meeting, UNFPA premiered a new video with testimonies of married girls. As one girl from Burkina Faso explains: "I was promised to a man before I was 10. It was a traditional wedding. When the time came, I was just handed over to my husband's family and when I saw him I realized he was older than my daddy."

Ms. Obaid called for greater action to protect the rights of married girls and stressed that child marriage brought great health risks for young girls. Pregnancy is a leading cause of death and disability for young girls aged 15 to 19. Married adolescent girls are at particular risk of HIV infection since they are often married to much older men with more sexual experience and are generally unable to negotiate condom use. Studies from Kenya and Zambia show that teenage brides are contracting HIV at a faster rate than their sexually active unmarried counterparts. An estimated 7.3 million young women are living with HIV/AIDS, compared to 4.5 million young men and nearly two thirds of newly infected youth aged 15 to 19 in sub-Saharan Africa are female.

The stakes are high. The largest generation of adolescents in world history is now making the transition from childhood to adulthood: 1.2 billion people are between the ages of 10 and 19. The health and well-being of young girls today will have a major impact on the overall social and economic health of our world tomorrow."

Madame la Ministre de la Santé (Health) Aminata Diallo from Senegal also took part. I believe I had met her, or at least her representative in Senegal. I showed her the wonderful booklet, with the seals of UNFPA and the Ministry of Education, which says on the front that little girls deserve as much food, education, and health care, as little boys. Senegal is really trying to be progressive and pro-active in spreading positive messages about the human rights of girls. And they have been successful in keeping down the rate of HIV infections.

I also attended a smaller panel on PAC in Kenya. PAC is post abortion care. The program in Kenya is called COBAC, Community Based Abortion Care. There are 6000 deaths each year in Kenya due to illegal abortion, half among very young women. They often die in the rainy season because there is no transportation to health clinics available. The ground is impassable.

I hope you will be shocked by what I am going to write: *For the first time in 30 years the US Agency for International Development and Health and Human Services (HHS) did not offer any financial support for this conference.* Not only did the US break with tradition by not offering any funding for this conference, but it also ordered physicians and health professionals under its control not to attend. The reason? UNFPA's presence, and perhaps also the presence of the International Planned Parenthood Federation which has refused to adhere to the Gag Rule. Here are some words from

Dr. Nils Daulaire, M.D., President and CEO of the Global Health Council:

"Let me be clear: the people who have driven a wedge between US public health officials and their colleagues at this conference are not concerned with solving worldwide health threats. Their concerns are elsewhere. No, these extremists limited their research to finding, on our preliminary conference program, two organizations they consider objectionable because they will not bow to their hard-line anti-abortion positions. The wide-ranging work of IPPF (International Planned Parenthood Federation), which has not been blackmailed by the Gag Rule, and of UNFPA includes programs that are, from a public-health services standpoint, well worth sharing and discussing. They belong in this conference.

"But this clique condemns these organizations because one has not been willing to agree to the so-called Mexico City Policy—also known as the Global Gag Rule—and the other continues to work with humane health programs in China, despite the Chinese government's lamentable policies. These extremists deliberately distorted the realities of these organizations' participation at this conference, and cited another that is not even still on the program, in order to give their attacks news-making potency. They were not interested in the facts then, and after their stories surfaced and we sought to correct their misimpressions, they just shouted all the louder.

"Like extremists everywhere, they wanted to remove any possibility of a moderate middle ground. They wanted to disrupt the civil dialogue required for real understanding, which often results in thoughtful compromise. They wanted to discredit those who champion openness, because fair and thoughtful debate threatens their intention to separate reproductive health out from the rest of the global health agenda. And we will not let that happen. As if we could responsibly discuss youth without including reproductive health.

"For a health professional this is outrageous. But we should not be surprised—because that is what extremists do.

"What was surprising—and deeply disappointing—was that our government's health policy leaders did not respond with the truth. We will not be deterred, and we will not be gagged."

Those are pretty strong remarks by Dr. Daulaire. Lois and I are not alone!

Connecticut has been wonderful, and I've traveled there twice. Luckily you can criss-cross the state in a couple of hours so I've spoken at Eastern Connecticut, at Southern Connecticut, at U CONN, at AAUW chapters, and in Willimantic, had an hour and a half radio interview with Wayne Norman. 34 Million Friends and weather and sports all mixed up together.

Donna Collins was Executive Coordinator of the 2004 Gather the Women International Conference in Dallas, Texas. She had had a fistula during childbirth that her doctor had taken a long time to diagnose. So she was very eager to have me as one of the speakers.

Gather the Women was different from anything I had ever experienced. About two hundred women from all over the US and from abroad gathered to share their spirituality and goodness. I heard a song there, sung by Jana Stanfield. The words are haunting. "I can not do all the good that the world needs, but the world needs all the good that I can do." I also began a wonderful relationship with the Israeli poet Ada Aharoni who has established the International Forum for the Literature and Culture of Peace (www.IFLAC.org).

From the Gather the Women Conference I hopped to Madison, Wisconsin via Chicago Midway. Someone on the plane was reading a Dallas newspaper and I glanced at the headline: "Desperate Times" and I thought something awful had happened. But this was referring to a loss by the Dallas Cowboys!

Two days later on a flight to Columbus, Ohio from Minneapolis, I saw a woman in the row in front of me across the aisle reading a Molly Ivins column in the *Minneapolis Star Tribune*. So, when we were deplaning, I tapped her on the shoulder and asked if she were a fan of Molly Ivins and if she was, had she heard about 34 Million Friends. —Well, serendipity here, she turned out to be the daughter of former Senator John Glenn of Ohio of astronaut fame. She said she had sent more money to 34 Million Friends than she could even remember. She was on her way to a Kerry rally and her mother was meeting her at the airport. Big hugs. I gave her a DVD of the Odetta song and about 100 stickers.

I'm almost through with my Travel chapter. Bear with me. ... The Population, Family Planning and Reproductive Health section of the American Public Health Association had voted Lois and me a Special Recognition award in 2003 at the behest of Dr. Richard Grossman who had also been instrumental in my wonderful visit to Durango, Colorado. So I was back at APHA a year later to give an update. There were, in all, 13,000 people attending; the keynote address given by Erin Brokovich about environmental pollution and public health. She said "I speak to common sense." 34 MF speaks to common sense too.

One of the organizations present at the conference was ESRI, the multi-billion dollar Environmental Systems Research Institute which does global mapping with their own GIS software. ESRI is headquartered in Redlands, and has done population mapping for UNFPA. At APHA I spoke with Bill Davenhall, ESRI's Health Solutions Manager. He put a blurb in an international newsletter ESRI sends out about 34 MF linking it to the software UNFPA uses from ESRI.

And Larry Levine who is now national president of the United Nations Association (UNA) had me up around the Monterey Peninsula in California giving talks every ten minutes for about three days. —Only a very slight exaggeration!

And in late June and early July of 2005, Jay and I went to France to see very long standing friends in Grenoble, Marseille, and Clermont-Ferrand.   I spent our three days in Paris traipsing around, visiting UNESCO, which had something to do with our nomination for the Nobel Peace Prize as part of the 1000 Women Peace Project (www.1000peacewomen.org) and the Paris chapter of FAWCO, the Federation of American Women's Club Overseas. I also made contact with AFFDU (Association Française des Femmes Diplômées d'Université, the French AAUW), and with Reid Hall which headquarters several American campuses for study abroad. I dropped materials off at the American Church in Paris on the Quai d'Orsay and at the Mouvement Français pour le Planning Familial.

In all I've visited at least 18 states, 5 foreign countries, and 35 US colleges and universities. Unbelievable.

There, I'm done with my travels and I haven't even told the half of it!

Photo: Thoraya Obaid, in an address to a special meeting of the United Nations General Assembly, marking the Cairo consensus' tenth anniversary. *Credit: United Nations Photo.*

Chapter 14
Costs of Reproductive Health Commodities and Services

I thought you might be curious as to the costs of some commodities and services in the area of reproductive health. I'm just including the charts in US dollars, not the charts in euros.

UNFPA GLOBAL POPULATION POLICY UPDATE
Issue # 39
27 August 2004

This issue of the UNFPA Global Population Policy Update features documents recently developed by the Technical Support Division (TSD) of UNFPA, entitled "What Does a Dollar Buy?" and "What Does a Euro Buy?" These documents were produced in response to a need for an advocacy and fundraising tool that would provide quick figures on reproductive health commodity procurement and services.

They include easy to understand numbers on the amount of money needed, in both dollar and euro terms, to provide specific reproductive health supplies or to achieve certain outcomes, for instance, how much it costs to equip a referral facility for the provision of obstetric care, or how much it costs to prevent one HIV infection in a newborn, among others.

It is hoped that the documents would serve as a menu from which UNFPA and its partners would be able to pick specific information for use in advocacy and fundraising campaigns.

What Does a Dollar Buy?

Cost of Selected Reproductive Health Commodities and Services (2003 $US)

Family Planning

$0.02	Cost of one male condom (commodity cost only)
$0.15	Cost per male condom (distributed in a social marketing program)
$0.40	Cost of one IUD, providing a couple with protection against unintended pregnancy for (on average) three and a half years
$0.60	Cost of one female condom (commodity cost only)
$2	Provides one couple with contraceptive protection for one year using (male) condoms
$4.50	Enable a woman to avoid or postpone pregnancy for one year using oral contraceptives
$10	Enable 3 women to space their children using injectable contraception

Maternal and Newborn Health

$0.02	To provide preventive eye care to a newborn against blindness from neonatal ophthalmia
$3	Cost of one insecticide-treated mosquito net (to prevent malaria infection in pregnant women)
$5	Average cost of providing one pregnant woman with quality antenatal care

$10	Clean birthing kits for 9 women
$17	Drugs to treat a pregnant woman infected with malaria
$65	Average cost to provide a C-section (personnel cost, drugs and supplies)
$500	Provide a referral-level facility with the medical equipment and instruments needed to provide emergency obstetric care to a population of 150,000
$1,000	Cost of drugs, supplies and equipment required to provide care at the referral level to 36 women suffering from obstetric complications (i.e., back-up capacity to provide EmOC for 500 pregnancies

HIV / AIDS and other STIs
What Does $10 Buy?

$0.05	Cost of a syphilis test (test only)
$0.30	Cost of drugs required to treat one case of gonorrhea or syphilis
$0.80	Cost of an HIV test (test only)
$2	Enable a man to prevent STI or HIV infections for one *year* using condoms
$12	Cost per person receiving testing and counseling for HIV in a voluntary counseling and testing (VCT) program
$80	Cost of drugs required to prevent mother-to-child transmission of HIV
$150	Cost per teacher trained to educate students about HIV / AIDS and its prevention

What Does $1,000 Buy?

500	Male condoms
500	Newborns provided with preventive eye care against blindness from neonatal ophthalmia
200	Persons tested for syphilis
67	Male condoms distributed in a social marketing program
33	Persons treated for gonorrhea or syphilis
25	IUDs, providing 25 couples with protection against unintended pregnancy for (on average) three and a half years
17	Female condoms
6	Safe delivery kits
5	Couples protected by condoms for one *year* (for prevention of unintended pregnancies and/or STI / HIV infection)
3	Women enabled to space their children using injectable contraception
2	Women provided with quality antenatal care

80	Persons tested for HIV and counseled in a VCT program
36	Women with obstetric complications provided with the necessary drugs and supplies
15	C-sections
13	Newborn HIV infections prevented
7	Teachers trained in HIV / AIDS education
2	Referral-level facilities provided with medical equipment and instruments needed to provide emergency obstetric care to a population of 150,000 each

Chapter 15
Things I want to Say

I want the ultimate message of this book to be my vision for the women of the world. The world is going backwards and forwards at the same time. For instance, in Iraq you read that they may want religious law to govern marriage, divorce, women's rights. —Woe to the women of Iraq.

I had to laugh this morning (August 1, 2005) at an article in the *Los Angeles Times* headlined "Oil Wealth Divides Iraqis." Joost Hiltermann, director of the International Crisis Group's office in Jordan which tracks Iraq was quoted: "Women's rights are very important, of course, but however they come out, (in the Constitution) it will not lead to civil war." The point being that Iraq might have civil war over who gets the oil revenues, but not over the fate of half the human race. That is a wonderful metaphor for the state of the world. Very few of the powers that be will go to the line for the world's women and girls. It's always "the rights of women are very important, but..."

I don't want to appear to be in constant conflict with the Bush administration, but honestly, I think people would be appalled at some of the stuff that is under the radar. ... And unless the United States is a leader in the fight for women's education, lives, and choices, won't the rest of the world have an excuse to go backwards? And choices surely mean a choice of whether or not to use family planning. Ellen Goodman is right. I don't think this Administration would state that people have a right to family planning.

Aren't movements to curtail women's choices anything more than the message that women really can't decide for themselves, that they aren't fully capable of moral decision-making, that they need to be controlled? Isn't this fight against reproductive choice in America, and I'm not talking just about abortion, but about family planning, and access to information, extreme? Isn't the Gag Rule, which prevents people from telling the truth to women who come to them, wrapping women up in a *burka* of ignorance?

And if we live in a free country, how can we allow religious doctrines of particular religions to dictate public policy? This is what is happening in certain cases. —Woe to us.

On September 4, 2003, The United Kingdom based *Observer* printed an article entitled: "US Halts Funding for African AIDS Programme."

The Reproductive Health for Refugees Consortium (now called the Reproductive Health Response in Conflict Consortium) is an AIDS-fighting consortium that works primarily in refugee camps and in areas of conflict. It consists of the American Refugee Committee, CARE, Columbia University's Center for Population and Family Health, the International Rescue Committee, John Snow, Inc, the Women's Commission for Refugee Women and Children, and Marie Stopes International. The US said that it would continue to fund the consortium only if the consortium kicked Marie Stopes out. Guess what? Marie Stopes runs family planning programs in China and cooperates with UNFPA. According to the article, "at no point has the State Department accused Marie Stopes of abetting forced abortions and sterilizations in China. It appears to be implicated by its association." The Bush administration was saying that if Marie Stopes was kicked out of the Consortium, our government would continue its funding. The Consortium refused to be blackmailed so no longer receives US money. —My interpretation of what the US is saying, tell me if I'm wrong, is that if any government abuses the human rights of its own people, then no help should come to that government from outside, because somehow that would be indirect support for that government's abusive policies. WHAT!???

Colin Powell wrote an Op-Ed for the *Detroit Free Press* on June 17, 2004 entitled: "US Won't Stand by While Human Beings Are Being Trafficked." To quote just a few lines: "Women and girls as young as 6 are being trafficked into commercial sexual exploitation; men are being trafficked into forced labor; children are being trafficked into wars as soldiers." And then in conclusion: "We fight not just for the victims, and potential victims of human trafficking. We fight also for ourselves, because we cannot fully embrace our own dignity as human beings unless we champion the dignity of others."

Secretary Powell, you are right about that! But what kind of dignity does a woman have being deprived of the reproductive health care and family planning she needs?

Some of the money that was supposed to go to UNFPA did go into anti-trafficking efforts. I wrote the following letter to the *Detroit Free Press* which wasn't published, but I think it makes a good point:

"One of the absolute root causes of trafficking is poverty, another being illiteracy, another is lack of family planning availability, another the low status of women and children. In order to please the extremist groups, this Administration has taken away money from reproductive health and family planning. It has refused for instance to release $34 million to the United Nations Population Fund which works on just those causes which lead to trafficking, i.e. illiteracy, burdensome pregnancies when the woman herself and her other children barely have enough to survive. UNFPA strives every day to raise the status of women and girls so they aren't subject to the temptations of whatever is said or done to entice them into work or sex slavery. One could say that anti-trafficking efforts treat more the symptom than the cause and certainly one should not sacrifice the one for the other which is what the Bush administration is doing. I am co-founder of 34 Million Friends of UNFPA, a grassroots effort seeking support for the United Nations Population Fund."

On March 17, 2004 the *Boston Globe* printed an editorial entitled: "How Bush Treats Women" which was highly critical. Arthur Dewey who was then Assistant Secretary of State for Population, Refugees, and Migration, and Ellen Sauerbrey who was the US representative to the United Nations Commission on the Status of Women defended the Administration in a letter printed on April 3. I found their last point to be outrageously misleading. "President Bush remains committed to the key Cairo Programme of Action goals of reducing infant, child, and maternal mortality and providing universal access to education." This sentence gives the impression to the uninformed that the Bush Administration was supporting the Cairo Consensus, whereas the keystone goal of Cairo was universal and affordable access to family planning and the Administration had voted against reaffirming Cairo because of this latter keystone goal.

As I've already mentioned, in Santiago, Chile, the Administration had been outvoted 22 to 1. A little sneaky! And, they couldn't get away with this stuff if we all were super-well informed, which I must admit takes a lot of time and motivation. One can't be super-well informed about everything.

If a TV image shows a poverty-stricken hungry child, many people will send their dollars. If a TV image were to show a poverty stricken hungry woman, people would be less apt to send their dollars. If you had one dollar to help, would you give it to the child or the woman? Most would give to the child. Which comes first, the chicken or the egg? I don't know. I think I would give it to the woman. The woman will take care of the child. The child can not take care of herself. When the world takes care of women, women take care of the world. But then of course the woman was once a child and needed care so it goes around in a circle.

The corporate or sports world will support efforts for children. For instance, just today, (8/10/05) I noticed where the Association of Tennis Professionals (the men's tour) was aligning itself with UNICEF, the United Nations Children's Fund. I congratulate them. But, would there be one chance in a blue moon that the ATP would raise awareness for UNFPA? Being associated with UNFPA would be *controversial*, so no way! OK, WTA and LPGA, what do you say? I'm with you!

Anyway, readers, you do see my point. Incidentally, UNICEF and UNFPA work closely together as they both do with the World Health Organization (WHO).

Almost every other developed country gives more than we do as a percentage of gross national income to development aid. We give 0.16 percent. The aim for developed countries is to give 0.7 percent. So when you hear that we are the most generous country, that is true in total sums, but not as a percentage of wealth.

I have not spoken enough about the environment and how population issues and the environment intersect. Global warming, chemical contamination of world waterways, and the probable shortages of clean fresh water for the 9 billion human beings to come, scare the life out of me. In 2004 OUR PLANET, the UN's Environmental Program magazine had an issue dedicated to Women, Health, and the Environment to coincide with the halfway mark of the Cairo Programme of Action. Lois and I were featured in an article entitled "Citizen Engagement".

To understand the seriousness of environmental issues, I urge people to research the Millennium Ecosystem Assessment (MA) Synthesis Report. Hundreds of top scientists from all over the world participated in this project. The published results got very little coverage here in the US. I also suggest that you log on to www.Worldwatch.org. The publications of the Worldwatch Institute are outstanding. And www.redefiningprogress.org is a wonderful web site. They have produced wonderful educational materials for schools on sustainability and and promoted the concept of an ecological footprint.

When I spoke at the Commonwealth Club in San Francisco, I went back the next evening to hear Lester Brown talk about his book Plan B: Rescuing a Planet under Stress and a Civilization in Trouble. It is very readable and talks about global warming, water, and population. He is the former head of the Worldwatch Institute and now heads the Earth Policy Institute. Lester Brown has endorsed 34 Million Friends.

Feminism is wonderful. It is simply the belief that men and women are human beings together. Everyone should be a feminist. American feminists, some of the greatest women and men I know, have fought the good fight for their entire lives for equality for women and girls in all realms, in all places. They have been strong supporters of 34 Million Friends.

A book club of women has met at my house on the second Monday of every month for perhaps twenty years. They have offered wonderful moral support for 34 Million Friends.

Paul, Boyd, John, and Irv were a twice-a-week tennis doubles foursome in Redlands and would invite me to replace any one of them who couldn't be there. These four good friends have always been eager for the latest news about 34 MF. ... Sore shoulders and broken foot bones have curtailed our activities.

My usual attire around town is slacks, a tennis shirt and a broad brimmed hat. I HAD gray hair. And to my way of thinking, my teeth WERE just a little too yellow. So I now have the nice light brown hair of my youth and a little bit whiter teeth and I bought a few nice clothes. —Ah, what we won't do for a good cause!

Above: Mali, Segou District health officials discuss how to encourage people to take advantage of reproductive health care.

Above: Jane and Dr. Miriam Cissoko, who loved to practice her English.

Chapter 16
Conclusion

This morning, 7/22/05, I received over *Planetwire Clips* an article summarizing the Lebanese Women's Network fight for reforming the Penal Code. Law 562 of the Penal Code in Lebanon permits men to kill female members or their family if the women have compromised the family's honor. Law 522 pardons a rapist or kidnapper if he marries the victim. Laws recognize adultery as a crime for women but not for men. The group characterized the Penal Code as "sick" and "discriminatory".

In much of the world, women are under the thumb of repressive, horrible laws, policies and customs, which unfortunately reflect societal outlooks. Women and girls are used and abused. Extreme poverty and powerlessness characterize their lives.

And then we have the government of our country making their lives even more difficult, adding to their burdens, playing domestic political games with their lives. As Lois says, "Why aren't we screaming?" —Well, I hope this book is a gentle scream, a gentle push to say ENOUGH!

What do I mean by a worldwide grassroots movement for the women of the world? I would like to see:

- At least 34 million Americans give at least one joyful dollar to UNFPA. Please take a stand.

- Those 34 million Americans drop a note to the White House asking the administration to show compassion. I'm sure everyone in the White House has educated their daughters like their sons and used some type of family planning!

- At least 34 million people from around the world give a joyful gift to UNFPA or to an NGO working in this same field of women's and girls' health and human rights. Two US NGOs doing fantastic work are EngenderHealth and Pathfinder International. The International Planned Parenthood Federation, Population Action International and the Population Council do great stuff. Within almost all countries there are country or local organizations. UNFPA partners with all of these.

- Conscious efforts to "speak up" when girls and women are "put down." Remember, that we are all of woman born.

- Everyone use the words "reproductive health" and "family planning" as part of their vocabulary when they talk about poverty, development, and population issues. Let's not mince words.

- People insist that their governments live up to commitments made at Cairo. In my opinion, unless we live up to the Cairo Programme of Action, we will never attain the Millennium Development Goals.

- Governments live up to the promises made at Cairo which would mean that education would be universally available as would reproductive health care and family planning. All babies would be wanted, loved, nourished, treasured.

- No woman or girl ever again have to resort to rat poison or a knife in the belly to abort herself. —I know personally about these two cases, the first in Bolivia, the second in Africa.

- No woman or girl ever have an abortion other than by a health professional in sanitary conditions.

- Laws against abortion be recognized as often harmful and sometimes fatal to the poorest most vulnerable women in the world.

- Men and boys take responsibility for the children they father.

- Men and boys be full partners in responsible child bearing and child raising decisions.

- Millions of men worldwide take a stand for the women of the world.

- Honest statements by political and world leaders of the real harm caused by Bush administration policies.

- Coverage by the media of what a planet with 9 billion people will probably look like.

- An honest examination of cultural and religious beliefs and practices in all societies which undermine the dignity, the full human rights and individual self-determination for the girls and women (and boys and men) of the world.

I have had every possible good fortune in my own life. Wonderful parents who prized education, comfortable financial circumstances, a husband and two children who have brought me much joy, good health, good friends. I am so grateful. And time, the great gift of time, at this latter stage of my life, to do what my heart calls on me to do. Where does my clarion call for the girls and women of the world come from? I don't know. But it is deep

within me, very deep. And this all sounds so pretentious that I have to laugh! But now I've quit laughing.

All over the world women and men are risking their very lives to fight this good fight. Speaking out where they speak out is dangerous. Entrenched habits and beliefs oppose them at every turn.

The Thousand Women Peace Project which nominated me and Lois for the Nobel Peace Prize as one of the 1000 Peace Women can not even publicly name some of these women whose lives would be put in danger. But as the Hunger Project's Joan Holmes said, and I will close with her words, "Gender discrimination is the greatest moral challenge of our age and we will be judged by history on how we respond."

Appendix

1000 Women for the Nobel Peace Prize 2005

Millions of women work day in day out to promote peace. They care for survivors, help with reconstruction, and initiate a new culture of peace. To represent these millions, it is the aim of the 1000 Women for the Nobel Peace Prize 2005 that in the year 2005 a thousand women shall collectively receive the Nobel Peace Prize for their efforts in pursuit of peace. This political prize will show that the work women do is valuable and exemplary.

With the exception of 12 women, since it was first awarded in 1901, the recipients of the Nobel Peace Prize have been men. In negotiating terms of peace, many more warlords than peace-queens make decisions about security, reconstruction and new political structures. This despite the fact that women constantly prove that, with their experience and competence, they can develop and put into practice sustainable peace programs.

Our focus is on women worldwide from all walks of life—e.g., the woman farmer, teacher, artist or politician—who devote themselves to a future free of violence. Their thousand strategies for constructive conflict management should provide important impulses for conflict research and peace policies. Through the full scope of this project, new peace networks will be established and existing ones strengthened.

Answers to some of the most asked questions concerning the nomination of peace women:

Who could get nominated?

In looking for 1000 peace women, we did not limit ourselves to crisis regions. Women who are not within conflict regions but are nonetheless engaged in striving for a peaceful future got nominated, as peace is more than the mere absence of violence. We have a broad concept of peace, based on human security, which includes nutrition, health, the environment, human rights, etc. The international Project team was seeking especially unknown grassroots women who do not exercise any coordination function, but do direct and active peace work within their own immediate regions. This did not exclude women known nationally and internationally. We want to particularly honor women who perform largely unnoticed background work and who therefore receive little recognition.

Criteria which every peace woman has to fulfill can be summarized as follows: "non-violence" long-term and sustainable work, "exemplarity and a sense of responsibility," altruism/ selflessness, "transparency and tolerance," justice, "legal and transparent financial resources"

Can the Nobel Prize be given simultaneously to 1000 women?

No. According to the statutes, the Nobel Prize can be awarded simultaneously to three individuals at the most, or to an organization. Therefore, in December 2004 three women got chosen to represent the 1000 peace women. It will be the job of the international Project team to make it clear that these three women are proxies for the other 997 women and will receive the prize in the name of all 1000. The 1000 women got proposed to the Nobel Prize Committee in Oslo on February 1, 2005.

Will there be contact between women nominated within the same country?

An important aim of this Project is national and international exchange and the networking of the various worldwide peace initiatives. It must be shown that women in different countries have to face the same problems. But the manner of dealing with these problems can vary greatly. We want to point out new and different ways of conflict resolution. A worldwide network not only facilitates cooperation, but also helps to solve problems and strengthen the concept of solidarity. It is important to us to make it clear that there are very many women who work daily to promote peace.

Why 1000 women?
Because 100 are too few for the millions who act courageously.

The Book

The book of the 1000 peacewomen demonstrates the work and visions of 1000 women. It describes the life and achievements of each woman, whether she works at the grassroots, nationally or internationally. The book is both a good read as well as a concise reference instrument for NGOs, relief organizations, governments, as well as peace and women's networks. It is being produced KONTRAST and internationally published in English by Scalo Publishing, Zurich, Switzerland, by the end of November 2005.

Approx. 2200 pages
Approx. 600 photos in black and white
Hardcover, 19 x 12,5 cm
To Purchase this book, go to:
www.1000peacewomen.org

In brief: The work for peace by women worldwide shall become conspicuous, comprehensible, convincing and communicable. In this way women and men in conflict situations will be encouraged to commit themselves to peaceful solutions.

The 1000 women did not win the Nobel Prize for peace in 2005. Nor did they stop their important work in the world. Women have been ignored too long, but they persevere. The idea of a peace prize for such women is inspiring to us all.

"Of course we are disappointed, as we had hoped very much that the 1000 women would be recognized for their untiring and courageous work in the cause of peace," said the initiator and Swiss politician Ruth-Gaby Vermot-Mangold, "but we are also proud that within less than three years we have brought attention to the outstanding work done by these women in the cause of promoting peace."

BECOME ONE OF 34 MILLION FRIENDS

We invite our fellow Americans to participate in 34 Million Friends of the United Nations Population Fund by logging on to www.34millionfriends.org. Or you can send tax deductible cash or a check (made out to Americans for UNFPA) to:

> Americans for UNFPA
> 34 Million Friends
> PO Box 681
> Toms River, NJ 08754-9922

People from around the world can participate at www.unfpa.org with a click on 34 Million Friends.

All royalties from the book will go to 34 Million Friends

If your name is included in what you send us, your name will go on the web unless you state otherwise. We would love to have your address and email too.

Please act today and suggest to family and friends to do the same. Send at least one dollar and Take a stand for the women of the world.

Thank you!